A Dynamic Study of Some Derivative Processes
in English Grammar:
Towards a Theory of Explanation

A Dynamic Study
of Some Derivative Processes
in English Grammar:
Towards a Theory of Explanation

Kazuo Nakazawa

KAITAKUSHA

Kaitakusha Co., Ltd.
5-2, Mukogaoka 1-chome
Bunkyo-ku, Tokyo 113-0023
Japan

A Dynamic Study of Some Derivative Processes in English Grammar:
Towards a Theory of Explanation

Published in Japan
by Kaitakusha Co., Ltd., Tokyo

Copyright © 2018
by Kazuo Nakazawa

All rights reserved. No part of this publication may be
reproduced, stored in a retrieval system, or transmitted,
in any form or by any means, electronic, mechanical,
photocopying, recording, or otherwise, without the prior
permission of the copyright owner.

First published 2018

Printed and bound in Japan
by Hinode Printing Co., Ltd.

Cover design by Shihoko Nakamura

Preface

The present book is a descriptive study of some derivative processes observed in English and their analyses are offered in terms of English grammar. The analyses are then seen in the theoretical perspective of Grammatical Dynamism. Grammatical Dynamism is a conceptual framework advocated by Kajita (1977, 1997, 2002, and elsewhere) that has a view such that as a child acquires a language in a step-by-step mode as he or she grows older, so linguists should construct a grammar of a language in the same mode: a grammar at a certain stage grows to be a new form of grammar in the next stage. These successive stages will ultimately end up as what we call an adult grammar. This view is in sharp contrast to the one that does not take into consideration the intermediate stages between the initial and the final stage of language acquisition. The latter view is, as it were, an instantaneous model of language acquisition in the sense that language acquisition can be viewed as if it finishes instantly. Or it may be called a static model because of the absence of gradual steps leading to the final state of grammar. This instantaneous/static model may also be called an output-oriented approach. Grammatical Dynamism, on the other hand, refers to those intermediate stages and thus is called a dynamic model of grammar, or, simply, a dynamic model. It may also be called a process-oriented approach. Cf. Kajita (1977, 1997, 2002, and elsewhere). This book comprises certain case studies and the relevant theoretical considerations within the framework of Grammatical Dynamism.

I have long been interested in how the process of construction extension is guided, or in other words, interested in what the general properties of the mode of extension might look like. I have tried to explicate the formal structure of this mode, and then have illustrated how instrumental, and indeed indispensable, the mode should be. The mode prevails in the analyses of PART II.

Focusing on a variety of linguistic facts ranging from certain phonological matters and some idiosyncratic syntactic constructions, to the matters of poetics, i.e. how to successfully interpret the intent of the poet, I have shown the considerable extent that Grammatical Dynamism can indeed accommodate. Of particular interest to the readers of this book will be the theoretical innovations I have put forth. There are two of them. One is the classification of linguistic facts, 'accidental gap' versus 'accidental hap': the former is something that is possible but nonexistent and the latter something that is improbable but existent. I have provided theoretical bases to this distinction and its related matters, e.g. the problem of "Why this form but not that one?" The other theoretical innovation I have put forth is modification of Grammatical Dynamism: I have modified Kajita's (2002) theoretical format and proposed a new one so that it can be in the form of a theory of explanation. The new format is essentially such that existence of grammatical property P' at a certain stage S_i $(i \neq 0)$ is a sufficient condition for the existence of grammatical property P before that stage, i.e. S_{i-1}, or, equivalently, that existence of grammatical property P at a certain stage S_i is a necessary condition for the existence of grammatical property P' after that stage, i.e. S_{i+1}. The linguists' task is to explicate and elaborate the contents of P and P'. In order to put this format on an empirical basis, we need to have the format coupled with a provision, which says that P' and P share at least a certain set of features. Part of PART II and PARTS III and IV are devoted to this type of theoretical discussion.

A few more words on the theoretical matters. Suppose that there is a state S_1 and subsequently a related state S_2. Suppose further that S_2 is actually the case, and that a somewhat similar state S_2' is possible but in fact is not the case. Under this condition, it is false to say that all the structural description regarding S_1 can only predict S_2 but no other states, e.g. S_2'. This is because it is only by chance that S_2 is true. In this case, some might be inclined to talk of probability: S_2 is highly probable, or far more probable than S_2'; the researchers' task then is to calculate the degree of this probability. This type of approach, however, which is counting heavily on the matters of pragmatic reality, i.e. "things did happen or not," does not, it seems to me, constitute a grammatical description proper. In other words, probability is one of the matters outside of grammar. Rather, it matters in pragmatics. For this reason, the thesis of this book is not in line with such ideas as probability. (Cf. the discussion on the frequency of *hectometer* in chapter 2.)

This book is a slightly revised version of my Ph.D. thesis submitted to Aoyama Gakuin University in November 2015. In publishing this work as it is now, I owe much to Kaitakusha Publishing, in particular to Masaru Kawata's editorship.

August 2018
Kazuo Nakazawa

Acknowledgments

It is a great pleasure for me to take this occasion to acknowledge my indebtedness to all those who helped me in various ways to complete the present work.

Decades ago I entered Tokyo Gakugei University, and I learned a lot from a host of professors there: their specialties ranged from English and American literature to philological studies to linguistics to TESL/TEFL. I am especially indebted to Taiichiro Egawa, Senjiro Hosokawa, Shunsuke Wakabayashi, Iwao Iwamoto, Takeichi Hazome, Tetsuji Akasofu, Yasumasa Okamoto, Shozo Shibata, Minoru Nakau, Masaru Nakamura, Akira Ikeya, Masatomo Ukaji, and Masaru Kajita. I also enjoyed discussions with many friends day and night: they are Kuniyoshi Ishikawa, Makoto Hasegawa, Takami Tsunoda, Masakazu Takahashi, Masato Ozawa, Akira Obata, Fumitaka Hiroi, Fumihiko Sato, Hiroshi Sakuma, Kenichi Ono, Hiroshi Ikeda, Toshio Yamaguchi, Mitsuo Matsuda, Kazuaki Fukui, Hiroshi Owada, and Takeshi Omuro.

I am grateful to Minoru Yasui, Minoru Nakau, and Shosuke Haraguchi, who kindly and patiently guided my study at the University of Tsukuba. All through my graduate years, both at Tokyo Gakugei and at Tsukuba, I got no small amount of inspiration from all the fellow students: they include Hiroaki Sakakibara, Katsuhide Sonoda, Masahiro Kayahara, Kazuhiro Ushie, Tsuguyo Kono, Takeshi Omuro, Noriko Yamanaka, Kazutaka Sasaki, Yasuo Ishii,

Shigeki Seki, Norio Hirota, Satoshi Mikami, and Naoshi Koizumi, to name a few.

Since the earliest days when I started teaching at Aoyama Gakuin University, I have been fortunate enough to have extremely inspiring colleagues. Space doesn't allow me to cite all professors of all disciplines. Let me confine the list to linguists and philologists: among them are Tsutomu Makino, Hidetaka Mori, Tamotsu Matsunami, Tsutomu Saitou, Minoji Akimoto, Hiroshi Yoshiba, Teruo Yokotani, Donald Smith, Peter Robinson, Kazuyoshi Yamanouchi, Shigeo Tonoike, Shinichi Takeuchi, and Eric McCready.

Last but not least, I have to thank my family members, Noriko, Kazushi, and Miki, for their long-standing support during the years of preparation of this work.

Kazuo Nakazawa
Aoyama Gakuin University
Tokyo, Japan
November 2015

Contents

Preface $\cdots\cdots\cdots\cdots\cdots\cdots\cdots\cdots\cdots\cdots\cdots\cdots\cdots\cdots\cdots\cdots$ **v**

Acknowledgments $\cdots\cdots\cdots\cdots\cdots\cdots\cdots\cdots\cdots\cdots\cdots\cdots\cdots$ **ix**

PART I Aims and Scope

Chapter 1 Levels of Description and the Target of Explanation $\cdots\cdots$ **2**

1.1. Levels of Description in Linguistics $\cdots\cdots\cdots\cdots\cdots\cdots\cdots\cdots$ 2

1.2. The Target of Explanation $\cdots\cdots\cdots\cdots\cdots\cdots\cdots\cdots\cdots\cdots$ 3

   1.2.1. What is 'Explanation'? $\cdots\cdots\cdots\cdots\cdots\cdots\cdots\cdots\cdots$ 3

   1.2.2. The Problem of "Why this form but not that one?": A Higher

   Order of Explanation $\cdots\cdots\cdots\cdots\cdots\cdots\cdots\cdots$ 3

   1.2.2.1. Kajita's (1977) Dynamic Model $\cdots\cdots\cdots\cdots\cdots$ 3

   1.2.2.2. Dynamic Model Revised $\cdots\cdots\cdots\cdots\cdots\cdots\cdots$ 3

1.3. Outline of the Thesis $\cdots\cdots\cdots\cdots\cdots\cdots\cdots\cdots\cdots\cdots\cdots$ 4

PART II Some Derivative Processes:
Case Studies of Construction Extension

Chapter 2 An Analysis of a Derived Stress Pattern:
The Case of *kilometer* in American English ·························· **6**

2.1. Introduction ·· 6

2.2. Facts and Analysis ·· 7

    2.2.1. Types of Stress Pattern ·· 7

    2.2.2. Type-Specific Stress Pattern ······································ 8

    2.2.3. Peculiar Behavior of *kilometer* ································· 8

    2.2.4. Analysis ·· 8

2.3. Discussion ·· 10

    2.3.1. Problems ·· 10

    2.3.2. Solving Problems ··· 13

2.4. Final Remarks ··· 14

    2.4.1. Logic of Linguistic Description ································· 14

    2.4.2. Other Cases Explained ·· 15

    2.4.3. Idiosyncratic Mutations ·· 16

Chapter 3 Epenthesis and a Mode of Extension ···················· **18**

3.1. Introduction ··· 18

3.2. Facts and a Mode of Extension ·· 19

3.3. Exceptions and the Logic of Extension ······························ 25

3.4. Conclusion ·· 28

Chapter 4 The Grammatical Naturalization and a Mode of Extension
·· **30**

4.1. Introduction ··· 30

4.2. Grammatical Naturalization (GN) ······································ 30

4.3. A Mode of Extension ·· 33

4.4. Analysis of GN ··· 34

4.5. Conclusion ·· 36

Contents xiii

Chapter 5 The Interpretation of Keats' *To Autumn*
and a Mode of Extension **37**

  5.1. Introduction 37

  5.2. Phonological Facts 39

  5.3. Analysis 39

  5.4. The Case for the Mode of Extension 43

  5.5. Conclusion 49

Chapter 6 The Genesis of English Head-Internal Relative Clauses
(With Appendix: The Intensional Qualification of
Quantification) **51**

  6.1. Introduction 51

  6.2. Putative HIRCs 53

  6.3. Genuine HIRCs 55

    6.3.1. HIRCs and Their Syntactic Characteristics 55

    6.3.2. Semantics of HERC and HIRC 61

  6.4. The Genesis of HIRC 63

  6.5. The Structure of the English HIRCs 65

  6.6. Other Data Explained 66

  6.7. Possible Counterarguments 67

  6.8. Theoretical Issues 71

  Appendix: The Intensional Qualification of Quantification **74**

    6a.1. Introduction 74

    6a.2. Three Types of Definition 74

    6a.3. Definition of Quantification 75

    6a.4. Consequences of Intensional Definition of Quantification 77

    6a.5. Summary and Residuals 84

Chapter 7 Water Finds Its Level: Derivatives Find General Rules **85**

  7.1. Introduction 85

  7.2. Exceptions and Regularities in Phonology 86

    7.2.1. Primary Stress Placement 86

    7.2.2. Vowel Quality 'Restoration' 89

  7.3. Exceptions and Regularities in Lexicon/Morphology 92

xiv   *A Dynamic Study of Some Derivative Processes in English Grammar*

7.4. Exceptions and Regularities in Morphology/Syntax ·················· 93
7.5. Exceptions and Regularities in Syntax ······························· 95
   7.5.1. Nominal Adverbial ·· 95
   7.5.2. Grammatical Naturalization ································· 97
7.6. Theoretical Issues ··· 98

Chapter 8   The *Dungeon* Construction: A Syntactic Hapax Legomenon
··· **101**
8.1. Regularity and Irregularity in Exceptions ······················ 101
8.2. The *Dungeon* Construction ····································· 102
8.3. Assumptions ·· 104
   8.3.1. Grammatical Dynamism ·································· 105
   8.3.2. Major Rules vs. Minor Rules ·························· 106
   8.3.3. Extensional Dependency ································· 109
8.4. Analysis of the *Dungeon* Construction ······················· 110
   8.4.1. *With*-Construction ····································· 110
   8.4.2. Adverbial Phrase Preposing ·························· 118
   8.4.3. Analysis ··· 120
8.5. More on the *Dungeon* Construction: Further Extension ·········· 123
8.6. Conclusion ··· 125

PART III   Dynamic Model Reviewed and Revised: Theoretical Issues

Chapter 9   Empirical Puzzles ··· **128**
9.1. Grammatical Dynamism ··· 128
9.2. Possible but Nonexistent Examples: Accidental Gaps ·············· 129
9.3. Improbable but Existent Examples: Accidental Haps ·············· 130

Chapter 10   Theoretical Puzzles ··· **133**
10.1. How Far Extension Goes and When to Stop ····················· 133
10.2. Grammatical Roudabout or Else ································· 134
10.3. Tautology ··· 136

Contents   xv

Chapter 11   The Revised Dynamic Model ·· **138**
11.1.   Dynamic Model Revised ·· 138

Chapter 12   Evidence for the Revised Model ····························· **141**
12.1.   Significance of the Revised Model ······························· 141
12.1.1.   Empirical Puzzles Overcome ······························ 141
12.1.2.   Theoretical Puzzles Overcome ···························· 142
12.2.   More on the Revised Extension Format ························ 145
12.3.   Simple Illustration of the Adequacy of the Revised Model ······· 145
12.4.   The Nature of Logical Implication ····························· 147

PART IV   Conclusion

Chapter 13   Towards a Theory of Explanation ························· **150**
13.1.   The Revised Extension Format as an Explanatory Theory ······· 150
13.2.   Summary ··· 152

References ·· **153**

Index ··· **161**

PART I

Aims and Scope

Chapter 1

Levels of Description and the Target of Explanation

1.1. Levels of Description in Linguistics

We assume four levels of abstractness of description in doing linguistic research. Cf. Kajita (1974: 167ff.). They are shown in (1):

(1) a. Linguistic Theory
    b. Grammar
    c. Language
    d. Data

(1d) is a collection of raw data, which include excerpts from written texts, interviews, grammatical judgments, and so on. (1c) is something that is abstracted away from (1d). Likewise, (1b) is something that is abstracted away from (1c). And (1a) is something that is abstracted away from (1b). Thus English Language, for example, is a collection of systematicities induced from raw English data, English Grammar is a collection of systematicities induced from English Language, and Linguistic Theory is a collection of systematicities induced from all grammars of human languages.

1.2. The Target of Explanation

1.2.1. What is 'Explanation'?

Assuming the abstraction hierarchy in (1), since Linguistic Theory rules the behavior of English Grammar, we say Linguistic Theory explains English Grammar. Likewise, since English Grammar rules the behavior of English Language, we say English Grammar explains English Language.

1.2.2. The Problem of "Why this form but not that one?": A Higher Order of Explanation

1.2.2.1. Kajita's (1977) Dynamic Model

In this thesis, I will first assume Grammatical Dynamism, or Dynamic Model, advocated by Kajita (1977, 1997, 2002, and elsewhere), and later I will modify it. There are, in my view, two major theoretical aspects in Kajita's dynamism: one is 'theory format,' as in (2):

(2) If the grammar of a language L at stage i, G(L, i), has property P, then the grammar of the language at the next stage, G(L, i+1), may have property P'. (Kajita (2002: 161))

The other is the 'guiding principles' about how derivative processes proceed, some of the keywords of which are *'be-based-on' relation, base, model, head-nonhead conflict*, and so on. For some of the 'guiding principles,' see Kajita (1977) and the references mentioned in the note 3 of chapter 8.

It seems to me that Kajita's theory format (2) is rather abstract, and the 'guiding principles' seem somewhat too specific, or particularly designed to analyze specific constructions. So I propose a mode of extension, which, in a sense, is 'tangibly abstract.' The mode plays a crucial role in the analyses of PART II.

1.2.2.2. Dynamic Model Revised

Kajita's formulation of extension is a source of great inspiration to a number of subsequent researchers, but I point out that there are puzzles, both empirical and theoretical, regarding the nature of the format itself. Thus I propose modification of the model. See PART III of this thesis.

Through this modification, I believe we could give one of the possible answers to the longstanding question: the problem of "Why this form but not that one?" That is, why this form is structurally predictable but ungrammatical; why we expect there can't be such forms, but in reality there are. Answers to these questions constitute a higher order of explanation. See Part III for the detail.

1.3. Outline of the Thesis

Part II is devoted to the case studies of some derivative processes observed in English. In other words, we view these processes as cases of consruction extension and we try to analyze them in terms of Gramatical Dynamism.

Gramatical Dynamism is a theory that holds the idea that language acquisition progresses step-by-step, which is termed a process-oriented approach in Kajita (1997), and this is in sharp contrast to the theories that take the view that language acquisition should be made possible instantaneously, which is termed an output-oriented approach in Kajita (1997). Assuming that Grammatical Dynamism is quite right on the track, we still see some room for improvement, i.e. in the way Kajita formulates the theory. Part III is a critical examination of Kajita's formulation and we will revise the format. And I give evidence for the revision there. Part IV is a conclusion.

PART II

Some Derivative Processes: Case Studies of Construction Extension

Chapter 2

An Analysis of a Derived Stress Pattern: The Case of *kilometer* in American English

2.1. Introduction

This is an attempt to investigate the logical relations that lie behind the linguistic description.[1] In general, the issue should be phrased as follows: whether a linguistic description for a phenomenon P should be a necessary and sufficient condition for P, a sufficient condition for P, or a necessary condition for P.

Empirical data will be drawn from the field of phonology, in particular the stress patterns of such words as *kilometer* in American English, simply because this is the area where the number of factors that would come into play is relatively small, as compared with syntax and semantics, when we make a linguistic description of the phenomena so that we would have easier access to logical discussions of the issue.

---

[1] This chapter is a slightly revised version of Nakazawa (1997). Nakazawa (1997), with slight modification, is reproduced with the permission of the Taishukan Publishing Company.

2.2. Facts and Analysis

2.2.1. Types of Stress Pattern

Of the words in English that have the morpheme {meter} at their end, we have four categories: one is exemplified in (1) as Group A, where the words included mean the units of length, and another is exemplified in (2) as Group B, the words of which group designate an instrument, device or gadget that determines the amount of the entity that is measured. (The marks on the vowel such as those in *á* and *à* represent primary and secondary stress, respectively.)

(1) Group A
   myriameter, kilometer, hectometer, decameter (Cf. *decámeter* in poetics), decimeter, centimeter, millimeter

(2) Group B
   algometer, altimeter, atmometer, barometer, chronometer, clinometer, ergometer, gravimeter, hydrometer, odometer, micrometer, pyrometer, salimeter, seismometer, spirometer, tachometer, thermometer, vinometer, viscometer

The third and the fourth categories are Groups C and D: the former comprises such terms in geometry as *diameter* and *perimeter*, and the latter such terms in poetics as *monometer*, *pentameter* and *decámeter*.

In this chapter, an analysis of the stress pattern will be made of the words mentioned above. And the basic phonological difference among the four groups of words lies in the distinction between Group A and the rest, i.e. Groups B, C and D. The words in Group A have a certain stress pattern, while those in Groups B, C and D have another, to which fact we will turn directly.

In what follows, I will be concerned mainly with the first two groups, i.e. Groups A and B, simply for expository purposes.

8   *A Dynamic Study of Some Derivative Processes in English Grammar*

2.2.2. Type-Specific Stress Pattern

What is characteristic of Group A is that each of the words in Group A has the stress pattern shown in (3), if we let the single dash represent a syllable or, more specifically, a vowel:

(3)   Group A: [´ – mèter]

Group B on the other hand has the characteristic stress pattern shown in (4):

(4)   Group B: [– ´ meter]

These are the basic facts on which our analysis will be made, and it should be noted furthermore that there are a couple of words that have an exceptional stress pattern in the group to which they belong.

2.2.3. Peculiar Behavior of *kilometer*

As far as American English is concerned, there is an item in Group A that has a peculiar behavior, namely the word *kilometer*, in that although it is a member of Group A and is pronounced *kílomèter*, it has a variant stress pattern like that of Group B, i.e. *kilómeter*. So, the question is: Why has the word *kilometer* (originally pronounced *kílomèter*) come to be pronounced *kilómeter* in American English?

Answering the question should involve a close observation of the words in Group B.

2.2.4. Analysis

In Group B, we have a number of words with a specific vowel stressed right before the morpheme {meter}, as shown in (5), where, and hereafter, we employ orthography instead of phonetic transcription where confusion does not arise:

(5)   Words of the type "... ómeter":
      algometer, atmometer, barometer, chronometer, clinometer, ergometer, hydrometer, odometer, micrometer, pyrometer, seismometer, spirometer, tachometer, thermometer, vinometer, viscometer

Chapter 2   An Analysis of a Derived Stress Pattern   9

Given the fact that *kilómeter* and the words in (5) have the same vowel stressed before {meter}, we see a certain relationship between the words in Groups A and B. Thus, using the notions and terms of Grammatical Dynamism initiated by Kajita (1977), we will answer the question posited in the previous section in such a way that *kilómeter* is derivatively obtained from the base form *kílomèter* on the model of the words in (5). Put differently, the process in question would be described as in (6), where, and hereafter, we assume that X is a vowel of any kind, that V is a specific kind of vowel, that a dash is a (possibly null) sequence of consonants, and that {meter} is word-final:

(6)   If we have [X-V́-*meter*] in one group of words and [X́-V-*mèter*] in the other group of words, then we have [X-V́-*meter*] in the latter group of words.

(6), a general statement, will have (7) as one of its possible instantiations:

(7)   If we have [X-ó-*meter*] in Group B and [X́-o-*mèter*] in Group A, then we have [X-ó-*meter*] in Group A.

(7) is a description of the phenomena, but at the same time we could regard it as an analysis that would make predictions. The analysis that we formulated in (7) is far-reaching in that besides *kilometer* it accommodates certain other words that should or should not have a variant stress pattern. First, according to *Webster's Third New International Dictionary of the English Language* (hereafter *Webster³*), we have *hectómeter* as well as *héctomèter*, which fact is a straightforward outcome of the analysis of (7). (It is interesting to note that while *Webster³* of 1965 edition records only the latter stress pattern, *Webster³* of 1976 edition shows both stress patterns.) For, *hectometer* is a word (and, virtually the only word in Group A other than *kilometer*) that has the vowel *o* stressed before {meter}. Needless to say, no other words in Group A have the form [X-V́-*meter*].

Secondly, because (7) explicitly dictates that only the words with the morpheme {meter} undergo the intended change, it predicts that words with other morphemes, such as {calorie}, {gram}, {liter}, {watt} and {watt-hour}, do not undergo the change, and this is borne out since we do not have the words in (8) with the specified stress pattern:

10   *A Dynamic Study of Some Derivative Processes in English Grammar*

(8) *kilócalorie, * kilógram, *kilóliter, *kilówatt, *kilówatt-hour

2.3. Discussion

2.3.1. Problems

Once the analysis in (7) is established, we could then infer that we could make similar predictions with a vowel other than *o* in the place of V in (6). Let us take the case of the vowel *i*. Following the version of (7), (6) would then have to be instantiated as (9):

(9) If we have [X-*i-meter*] in Group B and [X́-*i-mèter*] in Group A, then we have [X-*i-meter*] in Group A.

If (9) is correct, we would predict that we should have the words in (10) because we have *altímeter, gravímeter* and *salímeter* in Group B and *déciméter, céntimèter* and *míllimèter* in Group A. This prediction, however, turns out to be wrong.

(10) *decímeter, *centímeter, *millímeter

This is the first of a series of problems regarding the analysis of (6).

In the case of *kilometer*, the word in Group A is affected due to the models in Group B. However, as far as the type [X-*i-meter*] is concerned, the fact is that it is the words in Group B that are affected due to the models in Group A. So, (6) should be modified accordingly and instantiated as (11):

(11) If we have [X́-*i-mèter*] in Group A and [X-*i-meter*] in Group B, then we have [X́-*i-mèter*] in Group B.

(11) correctly predicts that we have *áltimèter* and *grávimèter* in Group B because of the words *décimèter, céntimèter* and *míllimèter* in Group A.

One might say that the variant stress patterns *áltimèter* and *grávimèter* may well have been motivated by such words as *álitùde* and *grávity*, respectively, in which the main stress is placed on the first syllable in both cases. But there being a word of a certain stress pattern does not always induce the change (intended or whatsoever) in the morphologically related words. Thus *péntagòn* does not induce the change from *pentámeter* to *péntamèter*, nor

Chapter 2   An Analysis of a Derived Stress Pattern   11

does *thérmostàt* the change from *thermómeter* to **thérmomèter*. Therefore, the existence of a morphologically related word with a certain stress pattern is not a sufficient condition for the item in question to conform to that stress pattern. Instead, it should be regarded as a (candidate for the) necessary condition for the item to under go the change. We will turn to the discussion of this kind in §2.3.2. So, in this context, we assume that (11) is responsible for the stress patterns *áltimèter* and *grávimèter*.

(11) made a correct prediction, but, at the same time, it incorrectly predicts that we should have **sálimèter*, which we do not have. The predictions made by (11), therefore, are partly correct and partly incorrect, which is the second problem regarding the statement of (6) because (11) is an instantiation of (6).

The third problem comes from the words in Groups C and D, where we have such words as *diámeter*, *pentámeter* and *heptámeter*. Putting the vowel *a* in the place of V in (6) will give the version in (12):

(12)   If we have [X-*á-meter*] in Groups C and D and [X́-*a-mèter*] in Group A, then we have [X-*á-meter*] in Group A.

(12) correctly predicts that we have *decámeter*, which is virtually limited to poetics, eventually a member of Group D. But, on the other hand, (12) also makes an incorrect prediction in such a way as to claim that we should have **myriámeter*, which we do not have.

The fourth problem seems rather serious. Why do we not have such words as **báromèter*, **clínomèter*, **thérmomèter* and others in Group B even though they should be based on the models *kílomèter* and *héctomèter* in Group A? Theoretically speaking, if (6) is possible, then another variant form (13) below should equally be possible:

(13)   If we have [X́-V-*mèter*] in one group of words and [X-V́-*meter*] in the other group of words, then we have [X́-V-*mèter*] in the latter group of words.

So the question is, why do we not have (13)?

Notice that as regards the fourth problem mentioned in the last paragraph, frequency does not count in this case. You cannot resort to the frequency of the words in question in daily use in such a way as to claim that words of higher frequency are more susceptible to the change in question. It might be

12   *A Dynamic Study of Some Derivative Processes in English Grammar*

true that *kilometer* is a word of high frequency and therefore it undergoes the stress shift, but *hectometer* is much less common than *barometer* and *thermometer* and is nevertheless susceptible to the change while the latter two words are not. *Héctomèter*, a word of low frequency, undergoes the change and becomes *hectómeter*, but more frequent words like *barómeter* and *thermómeter* do not undergo the change and remain as they are.[2]

Let us summarize the problems discussed in this section that have much to do with (6) and its related statements, i.e. (9), (11), (12) and (13):

Problem 1:   Though (7) makes correct predictions as we saw in §2.2.4, the analysis (9), the logically equivalent version of (7), incorrectly predicts **decímeter*, **centímeter* and **millímeter*.

Problem 2:   Though (11) makes correct predictions in cases like *áltimèter* and *grávimèter*, it incorrectly predicts **sálimèter*.

Problem 3:   Though (12) correctly predicts *decámeter*, it incorrectly predicts **myriámeter*.

Problem 4:   Why do we not have **báromèter*, **thérmomèter* and others in Group B even though we have models in Group A such as *kílomèter* and *héctomèter*? In other words, why do we not have (13)?

---

[2] Observe the frequency table below. The frequency of *hectometre/hectometer* is drastically lower than those of *barometre/barometer* and *thermometre/thermometer*.

	BNC	WBO	COCA
kilometre	248	309	28
kilometer	8	46	888
hectometre	1	0	0
hectometer	0	0	1
barometre	0	0	0
barometer	152	155	664
thermometre	0	0	0
thermometer	145	131	1846

(Data access: July 16, 2018)

Chapter 2   An Analysis of a Derived Stress Pattern   13

2.3.2. Solving Problems

What I will advocate in this discussion is succinctly phrased in (14):

(14)   A linguistic description of a phenomenon P should be a necessary condition for P.

If the general assumption of (14) is correct, then we have to interchange the antecedent and the consequent of (6) in such a way as to rewrite (6) as (15), where we tentatively used neutral group names G and H:

(15)   If we have [X-V́-meter] in Group G, then we have [X-V́-meter] in Group H and [X́-V-mèter] in Group G.

(15) will be paraphrased in more informal terms such that if we have [X-V́-meter] in Group G as distinct from the other members of Group G, the general stress pattern of the latter group being [X́-V-mèter], then somewhere else, in this case Group H, there should be a model stress pattern, i.e. [X-V́-meter], by which the change from [X́-V-mèter] to [X-V́-meter] is motivated. In other words, except for (linguistic and structural) mutations, there should be concomitant conditions ripe enough for a certain change to take place. And the linguistic description is the enumeration of these concomitant conditions.

It should be noted furthermore that there are cases where even though the concomitant conditions are adequately ripe, the item in question is reluctant to change, or in much more informal terms, it is up to the item itself to change or not. Words such as *sálimèter and *myriámeter, mentioned in the second and the third problems in §2.3.1, are instances of this case. Salímeter and mýriamèter might have changed to *sálimèter and *myriámeter, respectively, in the same way as altímeter and gravímeter have changed to áltimèter and grávimèter on the one hand and décamèter has changed to decámeter on the other, but they are in fact reluctant to do so.

Notice that if we take a linguistic description or analysis of a phenomenon P to be a sufficient condition for P, it no longer is the case that the item in question is free to undergo the change. Thus if the item satisfies the sufficient condition, it must change, and if it does not satisfy the sufficient condition, it must not change as far as this sufficient condition is concerned.

With regard to the first and the fourth problems in §2.3.1, the solution is drastically simple. In reality, we have no instances of *decímeter, *centimeter or *millímeter* on the one hand, nor *báromèter*, *clínomèter* or *thérmomèter* on the other. Therefore there should be no necessary condition or linguistic description for these phenomena. Recall (14), which implies that if we do not have a certain phenomenon, we do not have a description or any necessary condition for it.

As far as the nonexistence is concerned, we have two types of it. First, all the nonexistent words mentioned in §2.3.1, which are shown in (16), are instances of accidentral gap. Secondly, the words in (17) are instances of systematic and structural gap:

(16) Problem 1: *decímeter, *centímeter *millímeter
Problem 2: *sálimèter
Problem 3: *myriámeter
Problem 4: *báromèter, *clínomèter, *ódomèter, *táchomèter, *thér-momèter

(17) *kilócalorie, *kilógram, *kilómèter, *kílometèr

Then one may well ask in what way these different types of nonexistent words are to be accounted for in the framework of description that we are assuming.

The answer is that the words in (16) did not step forward to undergo the change for reasons God knows, while the words in (17) could not undergo the change because they simply did not satisfy the necessary condition, or put differently, there was no model on which the change is based. Therefore, the words in (16) are possible but nonexistent while those in (17) are impossible, i.e. structurally ruled out, and nonexistent.

2.4. Final Remarks

2.4.1. Logic of Linguistic Description

From the discussion made so far, we conclude that the general assumption (14) is tenable, which is repeated below:

(14) A linguistic description of a phenomenon P should be a necessary condition for P.

What seems to be of theoretical interest here in this context is Kajita's (1983, 2002) formulation of the dynamic and non-instantaneous view on the process of language acquisition. The relevant part of Kajita's formulation is (18), where superscripts indicate particular languages and subscripts, stages of acquisition:

(18) a. If rules of type Y are in G_i^j, then rules of type Z are possible in G_{i+1}^j. (Kajita (1983))

b. If the grammar of a language L at stage i, G(L,i), has property P, then the grammar of the language at the next stage, G(L, i+1), may have property P'. (Kajita (2002: 161))

(18) is essentially of the form (19), where A and B represent the relevant portions of the statement of (18):

(19) If A, then B is possible.

(19), on the face of it, gives us the impression that A is a sufficient condition for B. But, in fact, (19) is a collapsed statement of "either (20a) or (20b)":

(20) a. If A, then B.

b. If A, then NOT B.

The situations characterized by (19) and (20) are, by definition, one and the same, namely, from a set theoretic point of view, the one where B is properly included in A. So the situation will be given another characterization, i.e. (21):

(21) If B, then A.

It is now clear that contrary to what appeared at first, A is a necessary condition for B. Thus, we can take Kajita's view and formulation of language acquisition to be a support for the assumption (14).[3]

2.4.2. Other Cases Explained

In discussing the phenomena of excrescent [t],[4] a case of epenthesis,

---

[3] But we will see a critical examination of Kajita's formulation in Part III of this thesis.

[4] As to whether [t] or /t/, I will have no theoretical commitment on the choice of phonetic

16   *A Dynamic Study of Some Derivative Processes in English Grammar*

Nakazawa (1983a) noted some problems, both empirical and theoretical, that emerged when we seriously attempted to describe and analyze the phenomena. One of the problems is rephrased with minor modifications as follows (for the details of the phenomena and the problems, see Nakazawa (1983a, b) and chapter 3 of this thesis):

(22)   While words like *expulsive* and *impulsive* have an optional excrescent [t], which means that the relevant part of the word may be either [ls] or [lts], words like *compulsive, compulsory* and *ulcer* do not, which means that the relevant part of the word is [ls] but not *[lts].

(Judgments are due to *Webster*[3] (1965, 1976).)

When I wrote the 1983 papers, I could see no determinant factor that should distinguish the epenthetic group of words from the non-epenthetic one. But now in terms of our understanding of the linguistic description, i.e. (14), the phonological environment that we had thought would trigger the intrusion of [t] (i.e. the environment in the rule: "ls → lts / [+V, +stress] _ [+V, −stress]," if not stated rather roughly for expository purposes) is not a sufficient condition but rather a necessary condition for the epenthesis of [t]. Thus, words like *expulsive* and *impulsive* stepped forward to undergo the process of epenthesis but words like *compulsive, compulsory* and *ulcer* remained as they are for whatever reasons. Therefore, once again, the assumption (14) is confirmed.

2.4.3. Idiosyncratic Mutations

In the first paragraph of §2.3.2, I wrote that except for (linguistic and structural) mutations, there should be concomitant conditions ripe enough for a certain change to take place. When I said "linguistic and structural mutations," what I had in mind is a group of examples of a certain kind.

The syntactic construction in (23) might have a base form from which it might have been derived but there seems to be no concomitant condition that would permit or induce the very construction (23):[5]

---

or phonemic notation in the case of epenthesis.

[5] But see chapter 8 of this thesis.

Chapter 2   An Analysis of a Derived Stress Pattern   17

(23)   Into the dungeon with the traitors!   (Jackendoff (1973: 347))

In other words, if we note the special, idiosyncratic use of the preposition *with* in (23), there seems to be no model on which (23) is based.

Other candidates for the linguistic and structural mutation include the expressions in (24):

(24) a.   [kingdom come]Nominal
     b.   [cats and dogs]Adverbial
     c.   [catch-as-catch-can]Nominal/Adjectival

From a purely syntactic point of view, (24a) is not a noun phrase but it has a nominal function; (24b) is not a syntactic adverb nor an adverbial phrase but it has an adverbial function; and (24c) is not a syntactic noun phrase nor an adjective or adjectival phrase but it has a nominal or an adjectival function. All of the phrases in (24) may have the base forms from which they are derived, but there seems to be no model that would determine the very structure each of the phrases in (24) has.

So I call the examples in (23) and (24) linguistic and structural mutations, and these examples do not constitute a set of counterexamples to the general assumption of (14).

Chapter 3

Epenthesis and a Mode of Extension

3.1. Introduction

In this chapter, I will show that there is a mode of extension that governs the processes of certain peripheral linguistic phenomena.[1] The mode embodies two subtypes as in the following:

(1) TYPE A
   If an item *a* of the category X is in the structure S, then another item *b* of the same category X is in the structure S.

(2) TYPE B
   If an item *a* of the category X is in the structure S, then an item *b* of the category X′ is in the structure S, where *b* in X′ is the counterpart of *a* in X.

In what follows, I will be concerned with the application of these types of formulas to the empirical cases, namely epenthesis.

---

[1] This chapter is a slightly revised version of Nakazawa (2002a).

3.2. Facts and a Mode of Extension

Here in this chapter, by "epenthesis," I specifically mean the phonological process of the cases exemplified in (3):[2]

(3) answer: [ænsə] → [æntsə]
     chance: [tʃæns] → [tʃænts]
     fancy: [fænsi] → [fæntsi]
     sense: [sens] → [sents]

In the words of (3), [t] can be optionally inserted between [n] and [s]. This [t] is sometimes called excrescent [t] in the literature. The appearance of excrescent [t] is guided by the stress patterns as in (4), and I assume that (4) is optional.[3]

---

[2] The facts and analysis provided in this section are in part due to Nakazawa (1983a) and chapter 2 of this thesis.

[3] The rule schema "<A> B <C>" is an abbreviation of the two rules "ABC" and "B" that apply in this order. V represents a vowel. C_y^x means the sequence of consonants the number of which is x at most and is y at least. So, C_0 represents no consonant, or any number of consonants. X is a variable. # is a word boundary.

Nakazawa's (1983a) original proposal is (i), using Chomsky and Halle's (1968:176–177) classification and organization of phonological features as in (ii)

(i)   [+coronal, −voice] → [−continuant] / <[+stress, V]>n___C_0<[−stress, V]X>#

(ii) Table of Feature Composition Matrix for English Consonants

	y	w	r	l	p	b	f	v	m	t	d	θ	ð	n	s	z	č	ǰ	š	ž	k	g	ŋ	h
vocalic	−	−	+	+	−	−	−	−	−	−	−	−	−	−	−	−	−	−	−	−	−	−	−	−
consonantal	−	−	+	+	+	+	+	+	+	+	+	+	+	+	+	+	+	+	+	+	+	+	+	−
high	+	+	−	−	−	−	−	−	−	−	−	−	−	−	−	−	+	+	+	+	+	+	+	−
back	−	+	−	−	−	−	−	−	−	−	−	−	−	−	−	−	−	−	−	−	+	+	+	−
low	−	−	−	−	−	−	−	−	−	−	−	−	−	−	−	−	−	−	−	−	−	−	−	+
anterior	−	−	−	+	+	+	+	+	+	+	+	+	+	+	+	+	−	−	−	−	−	−	−	−
coronal	−	−	+	+	−	−	−	−	−	+	+	+	+	+	+	+	+	+	+	+	−	−	−	−
round	−	+																			−	−		
tense	−	−																						
voice			+	+	−	+	−	+	+	−	+	−	+	+	−	+	−	+	−	+	−	+	+	−
continuant			+	+	−	−	+	+	−	−	−	+	+	−	+	+	−	−	+	+	−	−	−	+
nasal			−	−	−	−	−	−	+	−	−	−	−	+	−	−	−	−	−	−	−	−	+	−
strident			−	−	−	−	+	+	−	−	−	−	−	−	+	+	+	+	+	+	−	−	−	−

(Chomsky and Halle (1968: 176–177))

20   *A Dynamic Study of Some Derivative Processes in English Grammar*

(4)   [s] → [ts] / <[+stress, V]>n____ C_0<[−stress, V]X>#

(4) is paraphrased as (5) and (6):

(5)   If the first vowel before the sequence [ns] is stressed and the first vowel after this sequence [ns] is unstressed, then [ns] optionally becomes [nts].

(6)   Otherwise, i.e. if the antecedent of (5) is not satisfied, it is the case that if there is no vowel between [ns] and the right-side word boundary, then [ns] optionally becomes [nts].

(4) correctly explains the epenthetic facts observed in the words below. The phonetic facts that I employed in this chapter are based on *Webster's Third New International Dictionary of the English Language* (G. & C. Merriam, Springfield, MA) and *Webster's Ninth New Collegiate Dictionary* (Merriam-Webster, Springfield, MA). The former is abbreviated as *Webster³*, and the latter as *WNNCD*. Hereafter, in the words below, we employ orthography instead of phonetic or phonemic transcriptions where confusion does not arise, and also we employ a system of stress representation such that *á*, for example, means the vowel of the letter *a* with a primary stress on it and *à* the one with a secondary stress on it, both of them being [+stress]; if there is no diacritic mark on the vowel, it is [−stress].

The words in (7) do not satisfy the requirement of (4) because they do not conform to the stress template requirement of (4), which means that (4) does not apply to them. So they don't have excrescent [t], as predicted.

(7)   a.   concéit
      b.   concéive
      c.   consístent
      d.   consúme
      e.   constráin

The most significant difference between (4) and (i) is that (4) assumes that epenthesis is a process of addition of a segment, whereas (i) assumes that epenthesis is a process of change of a feature on a segment. So, (i) correctly predicts that it is a process of assimilation since the segment before the segment affected is [n], which is [−continuant], and the segment affected becomes [−continuant]. In the text, I talk of epenthesis as an addition of [t] simply for expository purposes.

Chapter 3   Epenthesis and a Mode of Extension   21

f. constrúction

g. constrúe

h. monsóon (*or* mónsòon)

In (8), there is no sequence of [ns] in the words, but only the sequence of [nz], so (4) does not apply to these words even though they conform to the stress template requirement of (4). There is no excrescent [t] (or [d], for that matter) in (8), as predicted.

(8) a. Káynes

b. kínsman

c. léns

d. Wíndsor chair

In (9), no epenthesis is observed since [nz] is not a candidate sequence and, furthermore, the stress template requirement of (4) is not satisfied by the words in (9):

(9) a. bénzène (*or* benzéne)

b. Hínsdàle

c. Lónsdàle

In (10), the rule schema (4) correctly predicts the epenthetic difference in the following pairs: the words on the left satisfy the requirement of (4) and have excrescent [t], but those on the right do not.

(10) a. cóncentràte—concéntric

b. cònsolátion—consóle (v.), consólatòry

c. cònspirátion—conspíre

d. cónstitùte, cònstitútion—constítuent

e. cònsultátion—consúlt

In (11), the stress template requirement of (4) is not met by the words, so the absence of excrescent [t] is correctly predicted.

(11) a. cóncèpt

b. cónsìst (n.)

c. cónsòle (n.)

d. cónsòrt (n.)

e. cónstrùct (n.)

f. cónsùlt (n.)

g. pínesàp

(12) and (13) are the cases of (6), so the left-side words of (12) and the words of (13) meet the epenthesis requirement but the right-side words of (12) do not. This is precisely what we predict.

(12) a. expéctance—expéctancy

b. rélevance—rélevancy

(13) a. éntrance

b. ínference

It appears that if you only observe the words above, you might think that epenthesis is a rule that affects only the sequence of [ns]. But that's not true. It is notable that excrescent [t] is observed not solely in the sequence of [ns], but also in other sequences that are somehow related to [ns]. Nakazawa (1983a) assumed that the entire phenomenon of epenthesis could be contained in a single rule schema or in a very small number of rules or schemata. But now I assume that the entire phenomenon of epenthesis is a result of multiple extensions from the core cases to the peripheral cases. Now I turn to this topic.

The fricative [ʃ] is a palatalized version of [s]. If we follow the wording of (1), one of the extensions we are interested in is (14):

(14) If a voiceless coronal fricative [s] is in the process of epenthesis, then another voiceless coronal fricative [ʃ] is in the process of epenthesis.

Phonetically speaking, [s] and [ʃ] are "neighbors," so they share most of the phonetic or distinctive features with each other. Epenthesis appears to be extended from the sequence of [ns] to the sequence of [nʃ], and this is in fact the case, as you can see in the words below:

(15) a. convéntion

b. declénsion

c. Hínshelwòod

(16) a. Ánshán

b. kínshìp

Chapter 3   Epenthesis and a Mode of Extension   23

    c. móonshìne

    d. wíneshòp

(17) a. chámpionshìp

      b. Dévonshìre

      c. spórtsmanshìp

Our rule schema (4), with [s] replaced by [ʃ], correctly predicts the epenthetic sequence [ntʃ] in (15) and correctly excludes epenthesis in (16) and (17).[4]

The next extension is (18):

(18)   If a voiceless coronal fricative [s] is in the process of epenthesis, then another voiceless coronal fricative [θ] is in the process of epenthesis.

This prediction is borne out by the following facts:

(19) a. Córinth

      b. nínth

      c. mónth

      d. mónthly

      e. ténth

(20) a. bénthic—benthónic, bénthòs

      b. epénthesis—èpenthétic

      c. méntholàted—ménthòl

      d. sýnthesis—synthétic

In the words of (19), the epenthetic sequence of [ntθ] is possible, as predicted. In (20), the sequence of [ntθ] is possible in the words on the left, but it is not in the ones on the right, which is again what our schema (4), with [s] replaced by [θ], predicts.

Following the wording of (2), a third case of our extension looks like (21) below:

(21)   If an alveolar nasal consonant [n] is in the process of epenthesis, then an alveolar liquid consonant [l] is in the process of epenthesis.

---

[4] Notice that according to *Webster*[3], the slang for the word *conscientious objector* is either *conshy, conchie,* or *conchy.* The spelling of the latter two tells a lot about epenthesis.

24   *A Dynamic Study of Some Derivative Processes in English Grammar*

Though the consonant [n] is a nasal and the consonant [l] is a liquid, they have a striking similarity: they are both alveolar consonants. Observe the epenthetic behavior in the words below:

(22) a. élse
     b. fálse
     c. fálsifỳ
     d. fúlsome
     e. whólesome

(23) a. állspìce
     b. Alsátian
     c. whólesàle

(24) a. Míles
     b. sálesman
     c. Wélls

(25) a. fóolscàp
     b. Sálisbùry

(26) a. Wélsh (cf. the variant spelling "Welch")
     b. wélsh (cf. the variant spelling "welch")
     c. wélsher (cf. the variant spelling "welcher")

(27) a. fílth
     b. héalth
     c. stéalth
     d. tílth
     e. wéalth

In (22), epenthesis is possible, so we see [lts] in the words of (22).[5] In (23) through (25), epenthesis is impossible, so we have no [lts] in these words. In (26) and (27), we have [ltʃ] and [ltθ], respectively. All of this is predicted by the rule schemata (28), which are extensions from (4) with the consonant [n] in the environment replaced by [l].

---

[5] Observe the witty title of Ballmer (1980). I am indebted to Norio Hirota, who pointed out to me the latter title.

Chapter 3 Epenthesis and a Mode of Extension   25

(28) a. [s] → [ts] / <[+stress, V]>1___C$_0$<[−stress, V]X>#
     b. [ʃ] → [tʃ] / <[+stress, V]>1___C$_0$<[−stress, V]X>#
     c. [θ] → [tθ] / <[+stress, V]>1___C$_0$<[−stress, V]X>#

Therefore, epenthesis is the outcome of the processes of extension from the core cases, such as the intrusion of [t] into [ns], to the peripheral cases, where [t] intrudes into the sequences of [nʃ], [nθ], [ls], [lʃ], and [lθ]. And these extensions are guided by the mode identified in §3.1.

In Nakazawa (1983a), the author took pains to look for ways to generalize the consonants [n] and [l] in the environment of epenthesis, for you cannot uniquely identify [n] and [l] and at the same time exclude any other consonants by using the feature composition matrix, as for example in Chomsky and Halle (1968: 176–177). (See note 3 for this matrix.) In other words, [n] and [l] do not make a natural class. But now we have a new perspective such that epenthesis is not a monolith phenomenon that can be described by a single rule schema, but rather it is a type of state-composite phenomena obtained through a number of derivative processes guided by the mode of extension given in §3.1.

3.3. Exceptions and the Logic of Extension

Considering all those data given in the previous section, it appears that the mode of extension shown in (1) and (2), with the rule schemata (4) and (28) supplemented, will go a far long way to cover the entire phenomenon. But the analysis, as it stands, makes wrong predictions.

I have assumed that (4) is optional. But (1) and (2) dictate that if there is epenthesis in [ns], there should be epenthesis in [nʃ], [nθ], [ls], [lʃ], and [lθ], as well. The fact is that we have a few exceptions. See below:

(29) a. compúlsive
     b. compúlsory
     c. úlcer

(30) a. expúlse—expúlsion
     b. ímpùlse—impúlsion
     c. repúlse—repúlsion

(31) a. filthy
      b. héalthy
      c. wéalthy

Although the words in (29) all conform to the stress template of the rule schema (28a), they do not have excrescent [t]. In other words, the sequence of [lts] is impossible in the words of (29). In (30), the left-side words invoke epenthesis, but the right-side words do not, for all their observance of the stress template requirement of (28b). The words in (31) have the stress pattern eligible for epenthesis due to the observance of the stress template of (28c), but they fail to undergo the process. This is seriously interesting because the derivational bases for these words, i.e. *filth, health,* and *wealth,* have all undergone the process and obtained the sequence of [ltθ], as we saw in (27).

When I said at the beginning of §3.2 that the rule schema (4) is optional, I had in mind the cases where (4) is applicable but does not apply. The above are such a type of serious cases.[6]

The problem is how we could incorporate the notion 'optional' into the mode of extension presented in §3.1. The solution to this problem is suggested in Nakazawa (1997) (and in chapter 2 of this thesis).

Nakazawa (1997) has proposed that the linguistic description for the phenomenon P should be an accumulation of the necessary conditions for P. Formally speaking, (1) and (2) should be rewritten as (32) and (33), respectively:

(32) TYPE A
      If an item b of the category X is in the structure S, then an item a of the same category X is in the structure S.

(33) TYPE B
      If an item b of the category X′ is in the structure S, then an item a of the category X is in the structure S, where b in X′ is the counterpart of a in X.

To put this mode of extension into the more informal terms, if peripheral

---

[6] A milder case is, for example, the one where *fancy* is pronounced either [fænsi] or [fæntsi], as is described by *Webster³* and *WNNCD.*

Chapter 3 Epenthesis and a Mode of Extension   27

epenthesis is observed in the sequences of [nʃ], [nθ], [ls], [lʃ], and [lθ], there
should be the basic case of epenthesis in the sequence of [ns]. The latter is
the basic case of [t] intrusion because (i) [n] and [t] have the same point of
articulation, i.e. they are both alveolar consonants, (ii) among the coronal consonants of [s], [ʃ], and [θ], [s] is the closest to [t], and finally (iii) [n] and [t]
share the feature [−continuant], which gives easy way to the description of
epenthesis as a type of assimilation.[7] In order to understand the notion "optional," (32) and (33), or for that matter (1) and (2), can be reformulated in
more intelligible fashion. They are (34) and (35), respectively:

(34) TYPE A

   If an item *a* of the category X is in the structure S, then another item
   b of the same category X is *possible* in the structure S.

(35) TYPE B

   If an item *a* of the category X is in the structure S, then an item *b* of
   the category X′ is *possible* in the structure S, where *b* in X′ is the
   counterpart of *a* in X.

The crucial term in characterizing the notion "optional" is *possible*. On the
abstract level, (34) and (35) are of the form (36):

(36) If V, then W is possible.

(36) is in reality a collapsed statement of "either (37a) or (37b)":

(37) a. If V, then W.
      b. If V, then NOT W.

From a set-theoretical point of view, W is properly included in V. Thus, it
should be clear that V is the necessary condition for W. (The latter interpretation is what I call a 'loose' inpterpretation of (36). See §11.1 in chapter 11.)

---

[7] So, [l] is rather a marked environment for the intrusion of [t], since [l] is [+continuant]
and [t] is of course [−continuant].

3.4. Conclusion

Epenthesis is not a unitary, monolithic, static phenomenon that can be described by a single rule schema or by a very small number of rule schemata. Rather it is the result of cumulative processes of extension from the core cases to the peripheral ones. So, if one wishes to take epenthesis to be a single phenomenon, s/he has to collapse the consonants in the environment, i.e. [n] and [l], and s/he is destined to fail because [n] and [l] don't make a natural class. But if we take epenthesis to be a set of states arrived at through a series of processes guided by the mode of §3.1, then it is natural to assume that some of the resultant states might be mutually inconsistent with each other in certain minor respects. That is to say, though [n] is the 'assimilatory' inducer of epenthesis, [l] is the 'non-assimilatory' inducer of it. The reason is that, as I remarked in note 7, while [n], which is [−continuant], helps intrude the [−continuant] segment, i.e. [t], [l] is rather a marked environment for the process of [t] intrusion, since [l] is [+continuant] but [t] is of course [−continuant].

Furthermore, it is notable that there is a general tendency such that the more basic the phenomenon is, the more instances we have, and that the more derivative the phenomenon is, the fewer instances we have. This applies to the case of epenthesis. Thus we have the largest number of epenthetic instances in the sequences of [ns] and [nʃ], and we have the smallest number of them in the sequences of [lʃ] and [lθ]. This is reflected in the number of sample words of epenthesis in this chapter.

Another notable point is that when the phenomenon is more basic, the rule for the process is purely optional, but when the phenomenon is more derivative, the rule for epenthesis is sometimes prohibited. Recall the cases of (29)–(31), where [ls], [lʃ], and [lθ], respectively, are rather peripheral environments. All of these characteristics are some of the typical features of Grammatical Dynamism advocated by Kajita (1977, 1983, 2002).

It should be noted that the mode embodied in §3.1 can be understood as one of the possible interpretations of the theory format put forth by Kajita (2002).

(38)   If the grammar of a language L at stage i, G(L,i), has property P, then the grammar of the language at the next stage, G(L, i+1), may have property P′.   (Kajita (2002: 161))

Therefore, if the arguments so far are on the right track, epenthesis, together with its extension analysis, will prove to be against the output-oriented approach and will be in accordance with the process-oriented approach, one of the principles of which is (38).[8]

---

[8] But we will see a critical examination of Kajita's formulation in Part III of this thesis.

Chapter 4

The Grammatical Naturalization and a Mode of Extension

4.1. Introduction

This chapter concerns the analysis of Grammatical Naturalization from the viewpoint that embodies a mode of extension in linguistic description.[1] §4.2 briefly surveys the phenomena I call Grammatical Naturalization, and §4.3 touches on what is meant by the mode of extension. §4.4 is devoted to the analysis of Grammatical Naturalization, and the concluding section follows it.

4.2. Grammatical Naturalization (GN)

In this section,[2] I will outline the phenomena of Grammatical Naturalization[3] (abbreviated as GN).

---

[1] This chapter is a slightly revised version of Nakazawa (2004).

[2] This section is a modified version of §5.2 of Nakazawa (2001a). Nakazawa (2001a) appears as chapter 7 of this thesis with a slight modification.

[3] The term "Grammatical Naturalization" is due to Nakazawa (2001b). The facts about GN are from the same source. Traditionally, the grammatically naturalized adjective that appears before the noun that it modifies is called Transferred Epithet. Transferred Epithets,

30

Chapter 4   The Grammatical Naturalization and a Mode of Extension   31

Most generally speaking, adjectives modify nouns both syntactically and semantically, as in (1):

(1)   a red flower

where *red* modifies *flower* both syntactically and semantically. However, there are cases where an adjective modifies the following noun syntactically but not semantically at all. Nakazawa (2001b) has pointed out that there are indeed such cases, which he called instances of Grammatical Naturalization. Some of the typical examples of the phenomena are shown in (2)–(4). For the detailed illustration of this type of linguistic phenomena, see Nakazawa (2001b).

(2) a.   They drank a *quick* cup of tea.
    b.   They quickly drank a cup of tea.

$\qquad\qquad\qquad\qquad\qquad\qquad\qquad$ (Nunberg et al. (1994: 500, n. 14))

(3) a.   A neighborhood group locked *legal* horns with the Berkeley school district yesterday over renovations to a junior high school playing field.

$\qquad\qquad\qquad\qquad$ (Deborah Beccue, *The Daily Californian* Dec. 5, 1991)
    b.   In the domain of legal matters, a neighborhood group locked horns with the Berkeley school district yesterday.

---

however, include certain types of adjectives in addition to the grammatically naturalized adjectives. In Nakazawa (2001b) I have proposed that GN adjectives be derived from or related to the adverbial expressions, but as far as Transferred Epithets are concerned, not all of them are so derived or so related. Thus, observe the following examples and paraphrases:

(i)   the wicked wound thus given (= the wound thus wickedly given)
(ii)   Let us speak Our free hearts each to other. (= Let us speak Our hearts freely …)

$\qquad\qquad\qquad\qquad\qquad\qquad\qquad\qquad\qquad$ (*Macbeth* I. iii. 155)
(iii) The whole ear of Denmark (= the ear of all Denmark) is rankly abused.

$\qquad\qquad\qquad\qquad\qquad\qquad\qquad\qquad\qquad$ (*Hamlet* I. v. 36)
(iv)   In me thou see'st the twilight of such day As (= such a twilight of the day as) after sunset fadeth in the west. (*Sonnets* lxxiii. 5)

$\qquad$ (Examples and paraphrases in (i)–(iv) are from Ichikawa (1940, s.v. *Hypallage*).)
In (i) and (ii), the adjectives *wicked* and *free* are Transferred Epithets that are derived from or related to the respective adverbial expressions in the paraphrases, so they are also instances of GN. In (iii) and (iv), on the other hand, the adjectives *whole* and *such* are Transferred Epithets but they are derived from or related to the phrases that are not adverbial in the sense that I mean in (i) and (ii). So, Transferred Epithets encompass GN adjectives as a proper subset.

32   *A Dynamic Study of Some Derivative Processes in English Grammar*

(4) a. Sam kicked the *proverbial* bucket.   (Chafe (1968: 124))

  b. Sam kicked the bucket and it was in the proverbial manner.

The italicized adjectives in the a-sentences of (2)–(4) do modify the following nouns, but they never function as semantic modifiers of the following nouns. Semantically speaking, they rather modify the entire sentence or the verb phrase, acting as sentential / VP adverbials, as the paraphrases show; b-sentences are paraphrases of a-sentences. What is striking in these cases is that once the adverbial modifier is transformed into an adjective, this adjective climbs down deep into the syntactic object of the verb phrase and goes hand in hand with the head noun of the object NP, which means that this adjective mock-behaves as a modifier of the noun following it. This process is what we call Grammatical Naturalization, since this adjective, born outside the verb phrase, let alone the object NP of this verb phrase, has now settled in the new foreign land with no kinship around her at all. Notice that "to drink a cup of tea" in (2) is a free phrase, so it can be decomposed into syntactic and semantic components. Notice also that "to lock horns with (someone)" in (3) is a syntactically decomposable idiom, but its entire meaning is, some would say, decomposable; others would say, not decomposable. And notice finally that "to kick the bucket" in (4) is such a hard nut idiom that you cannot break it into syntactic pieces, nor can you into semantic pieces.[4] GN, nevertheless, happens in each and every corner of the verb phrases in (2)–(4).

Followong Nakazawa (2001b), we regard GN in (3) and (4) as cases of syntactic extension from the basic GN of (2). Once GN has become a possible syntactic process in the syntactic free phrases as in (2), it will be extended to apply to the cases of idioms that are syntactically decomposable, like the one in (3), and furthermore even to the idioms that are syntactically least decomposable, as in (4).

When put in the semantic perspective, GN is extremely exceptional in that the prenominal adjective has no semantic relationship to the following noun,[5] but when put in the syntactic perspective, GN is not surprising. GN

---

[4] As to the syntactic and semantic decomposability, see some of the forerunners on idioms in the generative studies such as Fraser (1970), Newmeyer (1974) and Bresnan (1982), among others. Kajita (1974) and Nunberg et al. (1994) are helpful in understanding the Gordian knot state of the idiom structure, where syntax and semantics are intertwined.

[5] Note that grammatically naturalized adjectives are so exceptional that they are not used

Chapter 4   The Grammatical Naturalization and a Mode of Extension   33

adjectives find their most comfortable place right in front of the noun: this is nothing but a syntactic regularity, namely, "an adjective modifies a noun that follows it." The example in (1) is the crudest instance of this regularity and the examples in (2)–(4) the sophisticated ones.

4.3.   A Mode of Extension

We assume that there is a mode of extension that governs certain processes of linguistic phenomena. For example, in Nakazawa (2002a) (=chapter 3 of this thesis, with a slight modification) I have argued that the entire phenomenon that I call epenthesis should be neatly analyzed in terms of both the mode of extension shown below and the logic about the description in linguistics.[6]

(5)   A Mode of Extension
   a.   Type A
        If an item a of the category X is in the structure S, then another item b of the same category X is in the structure S.
   b.   Type B
        If an item a of the category X is in the structure S, then an item b of the category X′ is in the structure S, where b in X′ is the counterpart of a in X.

(Nakazawa (2002a: 39))

---

as part of the free nominal phrases: the sentence (i) below is perfectly grammatical because this sentence (or VP) contains the verb *drink*, and when we have no action or process that deserves the manner *quick(ly)*, the phrase *quick cup* invites a disastrous grammaticality, as shown in (ii), simply because *a quick cup* is not a possible free phrase by itself.
   (i)   John drank a *quick cup* of tea.
   (ii) *There is a *quick cup* on the table.
   Similarly, while (iv), being derived from (iii), is perfectly grammatical, (v) is wrong because it contains an impossible free nominal phrase *more detail*.
   (iii) We will discuss this topic [*more* in detail] in the last section.
   (iv) We will discuss this topic [in *more* detail] in the last section.
   (v)   *We arrived at *(the/a) more detail* in the last section.
[6] The logic about the description in linguistics is roughly as follows:
   (i)   The linguistic description for the phenomenon P should be an accumulation of the necessary conditions for P.

34   *A Dynamic Study of Some Derivative Processes in English Grammar*

The mode of extension in (5) embodies two subtypes, Types A and B. In the next section, we will see how GN is analyzed in terms of this mode of extension.

4.4. Analysis of GN

Let us first see how GN is formulated in the syntactic free phrases. Observe the phrases in (6) and (7):

(6) a.   [$_{VP}$ visit occasionally]
     b.   [$_{NP}$ Det A N]

(7)   [$_{NP}$ an occasional visitor]

Suppose that there is a situation such that someone visits somewhere occasionally. When this activity is phrased in the form of a verb, i.e. *visit*, the adverb *occasionally* modifies the verb as in (6a). The Theme or Actor of the action in this situation can be phrased in the nominal form as *visitor*, as in (7). In the nominal construction like (7), the adjective *occasional* modifies the Theme of this situation, i.e. *visitor*, which is due to the syntactic template of (6b). Notice that in (7) the prenominal adjective has a semantic relationship with the noun that follows it. The verb-adverbial modifier relationship in (6a) is suppressed in the adjective-noun structure of (7). This is the basic characterization of GN.

Now observe (8):

(8) a.   A sailor strolled by occasionally.
     b.   An occasional sailor strolled by.   (Bolinger (1967: 5))

Type A of the mode of extension (5) applies here. If an adverbial modifier (*occasionally* in (6a)) of the verb (*visit* in (6a)) in a particular situation becomes an adjective (*occasional* in (7)) that modifies the nominal Theme (*visitor* in (7)) of this situation, then another adverbial modifier (*occasionally* in (8a)) of the verb (*stroll by* in (8a)) in another situation becomes an adjective (*occasional* in (8b)) that modifies the nominal Theme (*sailor* in (8b)) of that situation. Notice that GN adjective *occasional* in (8b) is obtained through the mode of (5) and it no longer has any semantic relationship with the noun that

Chapter 4   The Grammatical Naturalization and a Mode of Extension   35

follows it, i.e. *sailor*, contrary to the basic case of GN in (7), where *occasional* has a semantic relationship with the noun that follow it, i.e. *visitor*.

Next, let us examine the case of (9), which is previously mentioned as (2):

(9) a.   They quickly drank a cup of tea.
    b.   They drank a quick cup of tea.

In (9a) the adverbial modifier is *quickly*, and in (9b) it becomes a prenominal adjective of the Theme of this situation described in (9). Note that the adjective *quick* in this case is no way related in semantic terms to the following noun, *cup*, only this adjective-noun string observes the rigorous syntactic template of (6b). This is what the basic GN and the mode of (5) predict.

The mode of extension is operative in the case of syntactically decomposable idioms. Observe (3), which I will repeat as (10):

(10) a.   In the domain of legal matters, a neighborhood group locked horns with the Berkeley school district.
     b.   A neighborhood group locked legal horns with the Berkeley school district.

In the situation where the idiom "lock horns with" is used as in (10), there is no real 'horns' involved as a participant of this situation: in other words, there is no concrete object that is purported to function as a Theme in the situation. So, Type B of the mode of extension is called for. If a Theme (*visitor* in (7)) of a particular situation has a prenominal adjective (*occasional* in (7)) that is derived from the adverbial phrase (*occasionally* in (6a)) of the sentence that describes the situation, then a Theme (*horns* in (10b)) of a figurative situation has a prenominal adjective (*legal* in (10b)) that is derived from the adverbial phrase (*in the domain of legal matters* in (10a)) of the sentence that describes this situation, where the Theme (*horns*) in this figurative situation in (10) is the counterpart of the Theme (*visitor*) of the concrete situation in (7).

The mode of extension is, furthermore, responsible for the GN in the most recalcitrant idioms, e.g. the case of "kick the bucket". Observe (11), which previously appeared as (4):

(11) a.   Sam kicked the bucket and it was in the proverbial manner.
     b.   Sam kicked the proverbial bucket.

36   *A Dynamic Study of Some Derivative Processes in English Grammar*

In the situation described in (11), there is no concrete object that should be interpreted as the intended Theme. But, in the world of the 'literal interpretation' of the figurative idiom "kick the bucket," the noun *bucket* functions as the Theme in the 'literally interpreted' situation of the idiom. So, the Theme *the bucket* in the figurative reading of (11) is the counterpart of the Theme *visitor* in the concrete reading of (7). Therefore, GN adjective is possible even in such a syntactically frozen idiom as "kick the bucket".

4.5. Conclusion

GN is possible even in the most frozen idioms as in the examples of (11) (= (4)), which fact has puzzled many idiom analysts, including Chafe (1968: 122–125), Nunberg et al. (1994: 508, n. 19), O'Grady (1998: 286), Pulman (1993: 252–253), and Fellbaum (1993: 278–280), among others. But these examples are indeed systematically obtained by way of the mechanism that assumes a mode of extension. Therefore I believe it is reasonable to conclude that the mode of extension proposed in the form of (5) has a sound empirical basis.

Chapter 5

The Interpretation of Keats' *To Autumn* and a Mode of Extension

5.1. Introduction

This chapter is an attempt to show that Grammatical Dynamism plays a role in the interpretation of poetry, specifically in the interpretation of John Keats' *To Autumn*.[1] In the course of our analysis, it is argued that the feature theory better contributes to the understanding of poems than the phoneme-based theory does. And Grammatical Dynamism characterizes part of the process where the lines created by the poet are interpreted feature-wise. It is our aim to shed light on the phonological import of the verses that we believe the poet intended to impart.

Grammatical Dynamism is a theory of grammar that has the following theory format:

(1)   If the grammar of a language L at stage i, G(L, i), has property P, then the grammar of the language at the next stage, G(L, i+1), may have property P'.   (Kajita (2002: 161))

Grammatical Dynamism conceives of a grammar as the outcome of step-by-

---

[1] This chapter is a slightly revised version of Nakazawa (2008). Nakazawa (2008), with slight modification, is reproduced with the permission of Hituzi Syobo Publishing.

step process of language acquisition. In other words, a grammar at a certain stage (except for the initial stage) is derived from the grammar in the preceding stage coupled with some other phenomenal but pertinent factors. For more details, see Kajita (2002) and the references cited there.

Now we see in the following the target of our analysis, the text of which is from Ogawa (1980: 244–245):

(2)   TO AUTUMN

I

SEASON of mists and mellow fruitfulness,
 Close bosom-friend of the maturing sun;
Conspiring with him how to load and bless
 With fruit the vines that round the thatch-eves run;
To bend with apples the moss'd cottage-trees,
 And fill all fruit with ripeness to the core;
  To swell the gourd, and plump the hazel shells
With a sweet kernel; to set budding more,
 And still more, later flowers for the bees,
 Until they think warm days will never cease,   10
  For Summer has o'er-brimm'd their clammy cells.

II

Who hath not seen thee oft amid thy store?
 Sometimes whoever seeks abroad may find
Thee sitting careless on a granary floor,
 Thy hair soft-lifted by the winnowing wind;
Or on a half-reap'd furrow sound asleep,
 Drows'd with the fume of poppies, while thy hook
  Spares the next swath and all its twined flowers:
And sometimes like a gleaner thou dost keep
 Steady thy laden head across a brook;   20
 Or by a cyder-press, with patient look,
  Thou watchest the last oozings hours by hours.

III

Where are the songs of Spring? Ay, where are they?
 Think not of them, thou hast thy music too,—

Chapter 5   The Interpretation of Keats' *To Autumn* and a Mode of Extension   39

While barred clouds bloom the soft-dying day,
And touch the stubble-plains with rosy hue;
Then in a wailful choir the small gnats mourn
Among the river sallows, borne aloft
Or sinking as the light wind lives or dies;
And full-grown lambs loud bleat from hilly bourn;   30
Hedge-crickets sing; and now with treble soft
The red-breast whistles from a garden-croft;
And gathering swallows twitter in the skies.

5.2.   Phonological Facts

In this section, we concentrate on the description and classification of the consonants that appear in *To Autumn*, allotting all consonants employed by Keats into either of the two groups, A and B.   Group A comprises /b/, /d/, /m/, /θ/, /ð/, /n/, /r/, /l/, /w/, /j/, /g/, and /ŋ/.   Group B comprises /p/, /t/, /f/, /v/, /s/, /z/, /š/, /ž/, /č/, /ǰ/, /k/, and /h/.   What characterizes the two groups will be made clear in the next section, where we show that the theme of each stanza is derived from, or closely related to, the phonological make-up of the stanza itself.

Table 1 in the next section is a table of classification and distribution of the consonants in *To Autumn*.

5.3.   Analysis

In order to interpret and appreciate the poem, we draw on a number of clues that surface as we analyze the verses.   The phonological aspect gives one such clue.   Now let us analyze the phonological make-up of *To Autumn*.

First, we see that the iterative use of the same sound makes it possible to create some poetic effect.   To take a few examples, /m/, /l/, and /f/ are effectively used in ll. 1–2; /m/ is iteratively used in l. 11; /l/ is the dominant sound in ll. 27–30, where some instances of /m/ and /n/ are interspersed among /l/'s.[2]

---

[2] In this chapter, preference is given to the feature theory over the phoneme-based theory.

These facts might fall in the phoneme-based theoretical analysis. In other words, these facts could be described in terms of phonemes, without recourse to features. For the very "same sounds, i.e. phonemes" are used iteratively in these lines. We notice in l. 21, however, that there are such "similar" groups of sounds as /p/-/s/ and /p/-/š/ (that is, *press* and *patient*), and find that their "similarity" cannot be described in terms of phonemes, for phoneme is the minimal unit and cannot be decomposed any further in the phoneme-based theory. On the other hand, the feature theory rightly describes this similarity, using the relevant features that are common to the pertinent sounds: /s/ and /š/, for example, share many features such as [−vocalic, +consonantal, −back, −low, +coronal, +continuant, −nasal, +strident],[3] and those features with respect to which they differ from each other are only two, i.e. [high, anterior]. Thus, as regards the difference, /s/ is [−high, +anterior] and /š/ is [+high, −anterior], which fact means that /s/ and /š/ are the same except for being either "alveolar" or "palatal" in articulatory terms. So, /s/ and /š/ are, as it were, "voiceless fricative neighbors." Thus, the feature theory accommodates the similarities, as well as the sameness, observed among the segments, i.e. "pho-

---

For ease of exposition, however, I employ a phonemic notation, using slashes, e.g. /m/, /l/, and /f/. I do not take up the notational issue in this chapter.

[3] For the distinctive feature composition of English segments, see Chomsky and Halle (1968: 176–177), the relevant part of which is shown below:

	y	w	r	l	p	b	f	v	m	t	d	θ	ð	n	s	z	č	ǰ	š	ž	k	g	ŋ	h
vocalic	−	−	+	+	−	−	−	−	−	−	−	−	−	−	−	−	−	−	−	−	−	−	−	−
consonantal	−	−	+	+	+	+	+	+	+	+	+	+	+	+	+	+	+	+	+	+	+	+	+	−
high	+	+	−	−	−	−	−	−	−	−	−	−	−	−	−	−	+	+	+	+	+	+	+	−
back	−	+	−	−	−	−	−	−	−	−	−	−	−	−	−	−	−	−	−	−	+	+	+	−
low	−	−	−	−	−	−	−	−	−	−	−	−	−	−	−	−	−	−	−	−	−	−	−	+
anterior	−	−	−	+	+	+	+	+	+	+	+	+	+	+	+	+	−	−	−	−	−	−	−	−
coronal	−	−	+	+	−	−	−	−	+	+	+	+	+	+	+	+	+	+	+	+	−	−	−	−
round	−	+																			−	−		
tense	−	−																						
voice			+	+	−	+	−	+	+	−	+	−	+	+	−	+	−	+	−	+	−	+	+	−
continuant			+	+	−	−	+	+	−	−	−	+	+	−	+	+	−	−	+	+	−	−	−	+
nasal			−	−	−	−	−	−	+	−	−	−	−	+	−	−	−	−	−	−	−	−	+	−
strident			−	−	−	−	+	+	−	−	−	−	−	−	+	+	+	+	+	+	−	−	−	−

nemes."

Now observe Table 1. This is a table of classification and distribution of the consonants used in *To Autumn*.

Stanza	Line	b	d	m	θ/ð	n	r/l	w	j	g	ŋ	Total	p	f/v	t	s/z	š/ž	č/ǰ	k	h	Total
I	1		1	2		3	3					9	3		2	5					10
	2	1	1	2	1	2	3				1	11	2		3			1	1		7
	3	1	2	1	1	2	3	1			1	12	1		1	2			1	2	7
	4		1		5	3	3	1				13		3	2	2	1				8
	5	1	1	1	2	1	2	1				9	1		4	3			1	1	10
	6		1		2	2	4	1				10	1	2	2	1			1		7
	7		2	1	2	1	4	1		1		12	2		1	3	1			1	8
	8	1	1	1	1	1	1	2			1	9			3	2			1		6
	9	1	1	1	1	1	3	1				9		2	2	3					7
	10		1	1	2	3	2	2				11	1	1		3			1		6
	11	1	1	3	1		3					9	1			4			1	1	7
II	12		1	1		3	2					7	1		3	2				2	8
	13	1	2	3		1	1					8		2	1	4			1	1	9
	14			1		2	4			1	1	9	1		1	2			1		5
	15	1	2		2	2	1	3			1	12		2	2	1			1		6
	16	1				2	3					6	2	2	1	2			1		8
	17		2	1	3		2	2	1			11	2	2		2			1	1	8
	18		2	2	3	2	3					12	1	1	3	6			1		12
	19		2	2	1	2	2				1	10	1		2	3			2		8
	20	1	3		1	1	3					9			1	2			2	1	6
	21	1	1		1	1	2	1				7	2		1	2	1		1		7
	22	1			2	1	1				1	6			2	6	1				9
III	23				2		1	2			2	7	1	1		3					5
	24			2	4	1				1	1	9	1		3	2			2	1	9
	25	2	3	1	1		3	1			1	12	1		1	2			1		5
	26	1	1		2	2	3	1	1			11	1		2	3	1			1	8
	27			2	2	4	3	2				13	1		1	2			1		5
	28	1		1	1	1	3				1	8		2	1	2					5
	29		2		1	1	2	1			2	9	1	1		4			1		7
	30	2	2	2		3	7			1		17	2		1	1				1	5
	31	1	1		1	2	3	1			1	10	1		3	3	1		2	1	11
	32	1	2	1	1	1	5	1			1	13		2	2	3			1		8
	33		1		2	2	2	2		1	1	11			2	4			1		7

Table 1. The line-by-line occurrences of consonants in *To Autumn*

Now some words are in order here about characterizing the two groups A and B. Group A is a group of consonants that are more or less vowel-like. Group B is, on the other hand, a group of consonants that are much more consonant-like than the Group A consonants are.

Vowels are [+voice], and so are all of the group A consonants (except for /θ/). Vowels are syllabic, and so are /m/, /n/ and /l/ of Group A. While stops, fricatives, and affricates are nonsonorant, glides, nasals, and liquids are sonorant just like vowels are (cf. Chomsky and Halle 1968: 302). Notice that glides, nasals, and liquids are all Group A consonants. The consonants /f/, /v/, /s/, /z/, /š/, /ž/, /č/, and /ǰ/ of Group B are all [+strident], whereas all Group A consonants are [−strident] (cf. Chomsky and Halle 1968: 176–177). Thus we see that all Group A consonants are vowel-like and that all Group B consonants are consonant-like.

Now, observe Table 1 closely. It will tell us that there is some indication of tendency in each stanza of the occurrences of the consonants. In the first stanza, (ll. 1–11), the number is 9 of the lines where the occurrences of the Group A consonants surpass those of the Group B consonants. In the second stanza (ll. 12–22), the number is 5 where Group A surpasses Group B, and there are almost the same number of lines, namely 4, where the Group B consonants surpass the Group A consonants. Notice here in this stanza that we have 2 lines where the number of each group's consonants is the same, i.e. ll. 18 and 21. In the third stanza (ll. 23–33), it is again 9 out of 11 lines where the Group A consonants dominate the Group B consonants. In sum, the Group A consonants surpass those of Group B in the first stanza, but each group is comparable to the other with respect to the consonant occurrences in the second stanza, and finally in the third stanza, Group A excels Group B again.

These facts given in the previous paragraph strongly suggest that we can relate this phonological evidence to the understanding of the poem. We may say that the main theme of this poem is expressed in l. 1, "Season of mists and mellow fruitfulness." Extending this theme, the first stanza describes the richness of the season Autumn, the second stanza the visual impression of it, and the third stanza the auditory impression of it. The fact that in the first stanza the Group A consonants surpass those of Group B is suggestive of the theme of the poem, i.e. the richness, or the mellowness, of the season Autumn. Visual impression does not appear to be related to the choice of

Chapter 5   The Interpretation of Keats' *To Autumn* and a Mode of Extension   43

sounds, i.e. consonants. In fact this is the case in the second stanza, where the statal vision of Autumn is presented. Reading the second stanza, we feel as if we were watching a film featuring scenes of Autumn. But in the third stanza, the auditory impression of mellow Autumn is rendered comparable sounds; the Group A consonants excel those of Group B in the final stanza. Reading the third stanza, we feel as if we suddenly heard sounds of insects, birds, and animals around us while watching a film of mellow Autumn's scenery.

Here we have come to a point where we are able to explain in a natural way the relationship between the content of the poem and the sounds used. Thus, the first stanza, using more vowel-like consonants, describes the richness and mellowness of Autumn; the second stanza gives a statal picture of Autumn by means of the comparable frequency of the consonants in groups A and B; and the third stanza gives the auditory expression of mellow Autumn, again making use of vowel-like consonants far more frequently.

Now let us turn to the issue of which theoretical framework we should assume in analyzing the themes of the stanzas. In the phoneme-based theoretical framework, it is true that it is not entirely impossible to describe the close relationships between the theme of the stanza and the sounds used. But this could be done only by way of listing the phoneme each time it appears, because phoneme is again the minimal unit. The feature theory, on the other hand, enables us to describe what kind of sounds constitute groups A and B by way of noting the common features in each of the groups. Thus the feature theory could help explain what type of sounds should relate to what type of theme in a natural way.[4]

5.4. The Case for the Mode of Extension

In an attempt to describe and explain the construction extension phenom-

---

[4] It should be noted, however, that this does not mean that I insist the phoneme-based theory be discarded entirely. On the contrary, I believe that the notion of phoneme is important and that it has some form of reality in our mind. The present chapter does not go into such (anti-)structural linguistic, if not psychological, discussions, but only points out that the feature theory makes a significant contribution to the interpretation and understanding of poetry.

ena, I have proposed in the previous chapters that there should be a mode of extension in the form of (3). In this section, I argue that the consonants in groups A and B are characterized in terms of this mode of (3).

(3) A Mode of Extension

    a. Type A

        If an item a of the category X is in the structure S, then another item b of the same category X is in the structure S.

    b. Type B

        If an item a of the category X is in the structure S, then an item b of the category X′ is in the structure S, where b in X′ is the counterpart of a in X.

The mode of extension given in (3) is a type of extension such that a construction appears in a grammar if it is based on an existing construction. In this sense, (3) is a type of mode that conforms to the format in (1).[5]

The mode of extension of (3) embodies two subcases, Type A and Type B. As an illustration of how the mode is responsible for the concrete cases, let us briefly see the analysis of epenthesis (cf. chapter 3 for the detail), before we start discussion about the consonants in *To Autumn*. Typical cases of epenthesis include (4), where /t/ intrudes between /n/ and /s/, this type of /t/ often called excrescent /t/ in the literature.[6]

---

[5] There may be other cases of extension, such as the one where a construction appears "out of the blue." For the latter type of cases, see Nakazawa (1999a).

[6] Note the following two cases of epenthesis observed in the printed material:

  (i) HILO HATTIE / 1¢SALE / *It Just Makes Cents!* [Underline is mine—K.N.] (*Spotlight Oahu* April 1–9, 1992 (A leaflet obtained in Hawaii, USA))

 (ii) (A couple visit a photo shop called *Happy Photo*)

      Clerk: Your pictures should be ready by Thursday, Ms. Grindstone...

      Lady: Great.

      Clerk: I hope you got at least one shot of you in that hat...it's awfully cute, if I may say so... [Underline is original]

      Lady: Gee, thanks.

      Clerk: At Happy Photo, we're not really happy unless our customers are happy, especially our personable, highly attractive customers... By the way, will you be wanting the jumbo prints?

      Gentleman: She's already got the jumbo prince, buddy. [Underline is mine—K.N.]

      (J. C. Duffy, "The Fusco Brothers" (A comic strip). *The Japan Times* February 27, 1993)

Chapter 5   The Interpretation of Keats' *To Autumn* and a Mode of Extension   45

(4)   hence   intense   since

Epenthesis of /t/ in the environment of /ns/ is extended to another case of epenthesis in the environment of /nš/ as shown in (5), where /nš/ becomes /ntš/, i.e. /nč/.

(5)   conshy[7]   extension   intention

Here, it is Type A of the mode (3) that is responsible for the extension regarding the environment of epenthesis: the environment for /t/ intrusion is extended from /ns/ to /nš/ as in the words of (4) and (5). If we follow the wording of Type A of (3), this extension is described as (6).

(6)   If a voiceless coronal fricative /s/ is in the process of epenthesis, then another voiceless coronal fricative /š/ is in the process of epenthesis.

By the same token, observing another set of instances of epenthesis in (7), where /t/ intrudes between /n/ and /θ/, we can account for the extension as in (8).

(7)   epenthesis   month   ninth

(8)   If a voiceless coronal fricative /s/ is in the process of epenthesis, then another voiceless coronal fricative /θ/ is in the process of epenthesis.

Next, we see the Type B extension in the following cases of epenthesis:

(9)   else   false[8]   wholesome

In the case of (i), *cents* is punned upon *sense*. Due to epenthesis, *sense* /sens/ becomes /sents/, which is identical to *cents* /sents/. This is one good piece of evidence that we have the process epenthesis. In the case of (ii), *prince* is punned upon *prints*. Due to epenthesis, *prince* /prins/ becomes /prints/, which is identical to *prints* /prints/. This is another good piece of evidence that we have the process epenthesis.

In chapters other than this chapter, I occasionally employ the term 'excrescent [t]' rather than 'excrescent /t/.' But I do not intend to mean any theoretical nor empirical difference between them, at least in the arguments made in this thesis.

[7] Note the variant forms of spelling for this word, i.e. *conchie* and *conchy*, which we have already noted in chapter 3. *Conshy, conchie* and *conchy* are cited in *Webster³* as the slang words for *conscientious objector*. The spelling of the latter two words, specifically in the form of -*ch*-, strongly confirms the existence of /t/ intrusion.

[8] Observe the witty title of Ballmer (1980) as we did in chapter 3. I am indebted to Norio Hirota for pointing me out the latter article. The jokingly phrased title strongly suggests the existence of epenthesis.

46   *A Dynamic Study of Some Derivative Processes in English Grammar*

(10)   Welsh[9] welsher[9]

(11)   filth health stealth

In (9), (10), and (11), we find /t/ intrusion in /lts/, /ltš/ (i.e. /lč/), and /ltθ/, respectively. This is the result of epenthesis and this type of extension can be formulated as in (12) if we follow the wording of Type B of (3).

(12)   If an alveolar nasal consonant /n/ is in the process of epenthesis, then an alveolar liquid consonant /l/ is in the process of epenthesis.

Notice that /n/ is an alveolar consonant of the category "nasal," and /l/ is an alveolar consonant of the category "liquid." Thus (12) is clearly a case of Type B extension.

So far, we have presented arguments for the mode of extension in (3): the process epenthesis is neatly described in terms of the mode. I have also argued for the mode in the syntactic analysis of what I call Grammatical Naturalization in chapter 4.

Now we turn to the discussion about the distribution of the consonants in *To Autumn*. Specifically, I argue that the consonants in groups A and B are characterized in terms of the mode in (3). The Group A consonants are vowel-like, whereas the Group B consonants are less vowel-like, i.e. more consonant-like.

First, regarding the Group A consonants, it is clearly the case, except for /θ/, to which we will turn shortly, that they are [+voice] as all vowels are. In this sense, the Group A consonants are vowel-like.

Next, we focus on glides, nasals, and liquids. While stops, fricatives, and affricates are nonsonorant, vowels, glides, nasals, and liquids are sonorant (cf. Chomsky and Halle (1968: 302)). If we put the latter fact into the Type A phrasing of the mode (3), it will be like (13).

(13)   If vowels of the "sonorant category" are vowel-like (by definition), then glides, nasals, and liquids of the "sonorant category" are vowel-like.

---

[9] Notice that we have the variant spelling forms, i.e. *Welch* and *welcher*. These forms of spelling, specifically in the form of *-ch-*, strongly confirm the existence of /t/ intrusion.

Chapter 5   The Interpretation of Keats' *To Autumn* and a Mode of Extension   47

Notice that if we simplify the formulation, (13) means (13′) below, where the value for the variable x is "vowels" or "glides, nasals, and liquids."

(13′)   If x is of the "sonorant category," then x is vowel-like.

(13′) will give a more straightforward understanding than (13) does about what is vowel-like. It is not that (13) and (13′) mean different things, but what they mean is the same: glides, nasals, and liquids are vowel-like because they are sonorant.

Thirdly, /m/, /n/, and /l/ can be syllabic, just like vowels are. This fact can be formulated in terms of the Type A phrasing of (3), as in (14).

(14)   If vowels of the "syllabic category" are vowel-like (by definition), then /m/, /n/, and /l/ of the "syllabic category" are vowel-like.

If we simplify the formulation, (14) means (14′) below, where the value for the variable x is "vowels" or "/m/, /n/, and /l/."

(14′)   If x is of the "syllabic category," then x is vowel-like.

(14′) will give a more straightforward understanding than (14) does about what is vowel-like. It is not that (14) and (14′) mean different things, but what they mean is the same: /m/, /n/, and /l/ are vowel-like because they are syllabic.

In the fourth place, among the features that distinguish the voiceless stops /p/, /t/, and /k/ from the voiced stops /b/, /d/, and /g/ is, typically, the feature [+ / −voice]. But there is another feature that divides the two groups, i.e. the feature that induces or prevents aspiration. Let us call this feature [+ / −aspiration].[10] Needless to say, all consonants other than /p/, /t/, and /k/ are [−aspiration], including glides, nasals, and liquids among others. This fact renders the formulation in (15), which is basically of the form of Type B in (3)

---

[10] Technically, what induces aspiration in English is not a segmental feature, but rather an "environmental" feature such that the environment in (i) induces aspiration.

   (i)   (Roughly stated)
         voiceless stop → 'aspirated' / # ___ [+stress, vowel]
But voiced stops /b/, /d/ and /g/ never get aspirated. In this chapter, I tentatively assume that /p/, /t/ and /k/ are [+aspiration] and that /b/, /d/ and /g/ are [−aspiration].

(15) If glides, nasals, and liquids, which are [−aspiration] and sonorant, are vowel-like, then /b/, /d/, and /g/, which are [−aspiration] and of the [−continuant] category, are vowel-like.

Finally, except for /θ/ and /ð/, all fricatives are [+strident], while glides, nasals, and liquids, as well as vowels, are [−strident].[11] The point of interest here is the fact that /θ/ and /ð/ are [−strident]. Thus /θ/ and /ð/ are vowel-like in the way that is formulated in (16), which is basically of the form of Type B in (3).

(16) If glides, nasals, and liquids, which are [−strident], are vowel-like, then /θ/ and /ð/, which are fricatives but [−strident], are vowel-like.

So far, we have argued that the Group A consonants are all vowel-like.

We now turn to the Group B consonants, which are all consonant-like, or less vowel-like. First, contrary to vowels, which are [+voice] and [−aspiration], /p/, /t/, and /k/ are [−voice] and [+aspiration], so they are less vowel-like and more consonant-like. Next, all affricates and fricatives except /θ/ and /ð/ are [+strident], but vowels are [−strident]. So, that group of fricatives and affricates are consonant-like. Thirdly, as for the fricative /h/, it is, in fact, given the feature [−strident] by Chomsky and Halle (1968: 177). However, in articulatory terms, /h/ is a glottal or pharyngeal fricative, and no English vowel is glottal nor pharyngeal. Furthermore, vowels are [+voice] but /h/ is [−voice]. Thus, we take /h/ to be less vowel-like, i.e. more consonant-like, and assign it to Group B. In the fourth place, vowels are sonorant, but all the B group consonants are nonsonorant. The latter group of consonants are, therefore, less vowel-like, i.e. more consonant-like. Thus far, we have shown that the Group A consonants are vowel-like, and that the Group B consonants are consonant-like.

Summarizing, in the course of this endeavor of classification, we took full advantage of the mode of extension in (3). Therefore, the arguments for

---

[11] According to the distinctive feature composition table given in note 3, /h/ is, in fact, [−strident]. If we take the formulation of (16) applicable to /h/, /h/ should be assigned the "vowel-like status." But, for the reasons given later in the text, I assume that /h/ is consonant-like. Vowels and glides are similar in that they are unspecified with respect to the feature [strident] in Chomsky and Halle (1968: 176–177), and we assume that assigning vowels and glides the feature [−strident] causes no contradiction.

Chapter 5   The Interpretation of Keats' *To Autumn* and a Mode of Extension   49

the classification of Group A consonants and Group B consonants made above constitute the case for the mode of (3).

5.5.   Conclusion

John Keats' *To Autumn* consists of three stanzas, and each of these stanzas has its own theme. The main theme of this poem is briefly expressed in l. 1, "Season of mists and mellow fruitfulness." Extending this theme, the first stanza describes the richness of the season Autumn, the second stanza the visual impression of it, and the third stanza the auditory impression of it. Our contention is that the phonological architecture is so deliberately built by the poet that the theme of each stanza figures quite naturally in the minds of the people who are reading the lines. Thus, the first stanza, using more vowel-like consonants, describes the richness and mellowness of Autumn; the second stanza gives a statal picture of Autumn by means of the comparable frequency of the consonants in groups A and B; and the third stanza gives the auditory expression of mellow Autumn, again making use of vowel-like consonants far more frequently than consonant-like consonants.

The type of interpretation of *To Autumn* exhibited above is achieved through the reference to the two groups of consonants, and the grouping of the consonants is the result of the extensive use of the mode of extension in (3). The mode of (3) is one of the possible realizations of the format of (1). Therefore, Grammatical Dynamism plays a role in helping classify the consonants employed in *To Autumn*, and the classification is directly related to interpretation of the poem.

The classification has resulted in two groups of consonants: Group A and Group B. From a theoretical point of view, there appears a question of how to define these two groups. In other words, there is a question as to whether it is possible to define these two sets in terms of necessary and sufficient conditions. The answer is it seems difficult to do so. Rather, it seems that members of each of the two sets, i.e. groups A and B, share family resemblance with each other. Family resemblance in this case means vowel-likeness and consonant-likeness. If this observation is correct, then the mode of (3) is instrumental in the analysis of family resemblance. Family resemblance itself is a very serious topic to address if we want to characterize our mental processes. It is definitely desirable to step further into the area called family resemblance, but the research goes well beyond the limited scope of the present chapter.

Chapter 6

The Genesis of English Head-Internal Relative Clauses (With Appendix: The Intensional Qualification of Quantification)

Contrary to the received view that English does not allow head-internal relative clauses, I point out that English does have such ones.[1] After giving a detailed syntactic description of the construction, we argue that head-internal relatives are made possible through three adjacent successive stages: first, the stage of head-external relatives, second, the stage of a bridge construction with double analysis available, i.e., there is a head-external relative that allows for a head-internal interpretation, and finally, the stage of pure head-internal relatives. This process is characteristically a type of extension in Grammatical Dynamism. It is shown, furthermore, that this analysis encompasses another domain of data and that it is theoretically rich and constrained.

6.1. Introduction

From a typological point of view, relative clause structure is divided into two types: head-external relative clause (hereafter HERC) and head-internal relative clause (hereafter HIRC). Japanese allows both types, as seen in (1)

---

[1] This chapter is a slightly revised version of Nakazawa (2006b). Nakazawa (2006b), with slight modification, is reproduced with the permission of the English Linguistic Society of Japan.

below (head is underlined):

(1) a. Taro wa   [[sara no ue ni atta] <u>ringo</u>] o   totte, poketto ni   ireta.
    Taro-Nom [[plate on   was] <u>apple</u>]-Obj took, pocket-Goal put
                                                                    (HERC)
    'Taro picked up an apple which was on a plate and put it in a pocket.'

  b. Taro wa   [[<u>ringo</u> ga   sara no ue ni atta] no] o   totte,
    Taro-Nom [[<u>apple</u>-Nom plate on   was] Comp]-Obj took,
    poketto ni   ireta.   (HIRC)
    pocket-Goal put
    'Taro picked up an apple which was on a plate and put it in a pocket.'   ((1a, b) are from Kuroda (1976: 269-270).)

It has been claimed, on the other hand, that English is a type of language that does not allow HIRCs, both from an empirical and a theoretical point of view. Thus in English, (2a) is the only permissible relative clause structure while (2b) is illegitimate.

(2) a. [$_{NPi}$ <u>NP$_i$</u> [$_{S'}$ WH$_i$ [$_S$ ...t$_i$...]]]   (HERC; Head is underlined)
  b. [$_{NPi}$ [$_{S'/S}$ ...<u>NP$_i$</u>...]]   (HIRC; Head is underlined)

As regards empirical matters, Comrie (1989) does not refer to English HIRCs, nor does Keenan (1985). And, as regards theoretical issues, Cole (1987) argues for the theoretical consequence of the nonexistence of English HIRCs. Kayne (1994: 95-97) is essentially in line with Cole (1987) in dealing with HIRCs. According to Cole (1987), there are four types of nominal structure that has a relative clause attached to it either on the left side or on the right side, as shown below:

(3) Left-branching structure with head on the right, i.e. a relative on the left
  a. [$_{NP}$ [$_{S'}$ ...[NP$_i$ (lexical)]...] [$_{NP}$ e$_i$]]
  b. [$_{NP}$ [$_{S'}$ ...[$_{NP}$ e$_i$]...] [NP$_i$ (lexical)]]   (Cole (1987: 284))

(4) Right-branching structure with head on the left, i.e. a relative on the right
  a. *[$_{NP}$ [$_{NP}$ e$_i$] [$_{S'}$ ...[NP$_i$ (lexical)]...]]
  b. [$_{NP}$ [NP$_i$ (lexical)] [$_{S'}$ ...[$_{NP}$ e$_i$]...]]   (Cole (1987: 285))

Chapter 6   The Genesis of English Head-Internal Relative Clauses   53

The structure of (3a) is exemplified by a Japanese HIRC like (1b), and the structure of (3b) is illustrated by a Japanese HERC like (1a). While English has a HERC based on the structure of (4b), it lacks a HIRC of the structure (4a). Cole (1987) attempts to explain this typological asymmetry by resorting to the principle (5):

(5)   An anaphor cannot both precede and command its antecedent.

(Cole (1987: 283))

In (3a) and (4b), an anaphor $[_{NP}\ e_i]$ does not precede its antecedent $[NP_i$ (lexical)], so (5) does not block (3a) nor (4b). In (3b), though $[_{NP}\ e_i]$ does precede the antecedent $[NP_i$ (lexical)], the former does not command the latter. So (5) does not block (3b). In (4a), an anaphor $[_{NP}\ e_i]$ both precedes and commands the antecedent $[NP_i$ (lexical)], so (5) blocks the structure of (4a). In this way, (4a) is the only structure that is ruled out by the principle (5).

It should be noted that Cole (1987: 285-286) would not adopt such structures as in (6), simply because if he does so, he would fail to account for the absence of English HIRCs. If the structures in (6) were adopted, the principle (5) would have no way to prohibit them, since there is no anaphor in (6a, b).

(6) a. $[_{NP}\ [_{S'}\ ...NP\ (lexical)...]]$
     b. $[_{NP}\ [_{S'}\ ...NP_i\ (lexical)...]\ [NP_j]]$ (i≠j)   (Cole (1987: 281-282))

Therefore, for the possible structures of relative clauses, Cole (1987) posits an adsentential head NP, either lexical or anaphoric, and concludes that HIRCs are in fact HERCs.

The aim of this chapter is as follows: first, we show that English does have HIRCs; secondly, we give a detailed syntactic description of English HIRCs; thirdly, we explore the process through which English HIRCs are made possible; in the fourth place, we try to identify the structural requirements for the English HIRC construction; and finally, we argue for the dynamic interpretation of the genesis of English HIRCs.

6.2.   Putative HIRCs

A number of linguists are in favor of the position that there is no English HIRC, but Nagahara (1990) and Takonai (1994) claim that closer observation reveals that there are indeed candidates for the English HIRCs or, at least, their look-alikes. Their examples include the following:

(7) a. John invited [you'll never guess how many people] to his party.

(Lakoff (1974: 321))

b. The police came bursting in the door and talked to me as if I were [I don't know what] and then looked in the bedroom.

(Nagahara (1990: 58))

c. He sat by the telephone for [he did not know how long].

(Nagahara (1990: 58))

The underlined phrases in (7a–c) are the heads of their respective bracketed expressions, so the bracketed clauses themselves may well be regarded as HIRCs. If this observation is correct, we would have to conclude that English should have HIRCs. But as Nagahara remarks on the grammatical status of these bracketed clauses (Nagahara 1990: 59), this construction looks as if it were forged by the extragrammatical, i.e. discourse-oriented, factors. In other words, we can analyze the sentences in (7a–c) in discourse-oriented terms, just as Lakoff (1974) and Tsubomoto and Whitman (2000) do. Thus, consider, for example, the structure (8a):

(8) a. He sat by the telephone for [some period of time, but he did not know it was x-long (how long)]

b. He sat by the telephone for [some period of time, but he did not know how long it was]

c. He sat by the telephone for [some period of time, but he did not know how long]

We may take (8a) as the base structure to be converted to (7c). Applying WH-Movement to the bracketed portion of (8a) derives (8b), to which Ross's (1969) Sluicing now applies. The result is (8c). Grammatical components are responsible up to this derivation. Next comes a kind of pragmatic reduction of the discourse, which suppresses the sequence "some period of time, but" in (8c). The outcome is (7c). If this way of deriving (7c) from (8a) is basically correct, then (7c) is no longer an illustration of a genuine HIRC. One reason for this conclusion is that in a genuine HIRC, the head should stay where it originally was, as is the case with a Japanese genuine HIRC in (1b). Clearly, the purported head "how long" in (7c) has been WH-moved from its original

Chapter 6   The Genesis of English Head-Internal Relative Clauses   55

position. For another reason, a discourse-oriented reduction rule has been involved in the derivation of (7c), which means that (7c) is not a product solely of the grammatical components, but rather of the combination of the grammatical and the pragmatic components. Consequently, we must conclude that (7a–c) are not genuine HIRCs.[2]

6.3. Genuine HIRCs

6.3.1 HIRCs and Their Syntactic Characteristics

In the last section, we have concluded that sentences in (7) are not instances including genuine HIRCs. So what are the genuine HIRCs? The answer is that they are the bracketed expressions in the following:

(9)   A friend of mine once passed out from heat on a downtown street, falling into the gutter. [The closest <u>anyone</u> came to him] was the man who leaned over, just as my friend was coming to, and said: "Hey, you're blocking my car."   (Royko (1987a, 1987b))

(10)   Mrs. Clinton did not manage to utter the magic words, "not true," and neither, really, has anyone else. [The closest <u>anyone</u> has come] is the ubiquitous Bruce Lindsey, who, rather early in the breaking scandal, was asked directly by the Associated Press whether Mr. Clinton denied having troopers assist any affairs. "Yes, he has," Mr. Lindsey responded.[3]

                  (*The Washington Times* (1993); *Sekai Nippou* (1993))

---

[2] There are a whole variety of exceptions to the grammatical rules, a few of which are (7a–c). Another case of exception to the grammar is the bracketed portion in (i), which will be of interest to those who are looking for regularities in what seems to be a case of anacoluthia or a nonce word.

  (i)   Prior to this past season, however, Medina had only 10 Major League homers with the Indians (six in 1988 and four in 1989). His agent, promoting the player's desire to work in Japan, sent a video tape to Japanese teams, and the tape contained 10 scenes: all of his big league homers and nothing else. He must be terrific if [that's all he does] is hit the ball out of the park all the time.   (Graczyk (1992))

[3] I am indebted to Takao Ito for this example.

56   *A Dynamic Study of Some Derivative Processes in English Grammar*

(11)   Michael Howard was in Delhi, defending arms sales to Saudi Arabia. Kenneth Clark was touring Latin America, touting for privatisation business for Britain's merchant bankers. Michael Heseltine was [the nearest any of them got to the heart of Europe], slamming Mr Blair from the Italian holiday resort of Amalfi. John Major, meanwhile, had his head in his fish pond in Huntingdon, trying to avoid the flak flying so wantonly around the world.   (*WordbanksOnline*)

In what follows, I will give a detailed syntactic description of HIRCs, i.e. features [A] through [G] that characterize this construction.

[A]   The head is internal to the relative clause.

The second sentence in (9) that includes a bracketed HIRC has a meaning such that "among those who came close to the man, Mr. X was the closest to him, and Mr. X was the man who leaned over." As is evident from this interpretation, the head of the bracketed clause is a human being represented by the phrase *anyone* but will never be something represented by the phrase *the closest*. The same type of interpretation applies to (10) and (11), as well. Thus I call these clauses HIRCs.

[B]   There are HERCs that share a family resemblance with HIRCs.

There are a group of HERCs that have a close family resemblance to HIRCs in that the surface word order is exactly the same between the two constructions, i.e., both have the surface form [[*the* + Superlative] + NP + VP]. But there is one crucial difference between the two constructions: while in HERCs, the head is [*the* + Superlative], in HIRCs the head is the NP that follows [*the* + Superlative]. Observe the following instances of HERC:

(12)   [The closest Miles had been to a job in three weeks of searching] had been as a kitchen helper in a third-rate, crowded Italian restaurant.   (Nagahara (1990: 123))

(13)   The Monte Carlo Challenge is [the closest anyone gets these days to recapturing the magic of the 1950s and 1960s] when it was regarded as one of the supreme tests of car and driver.   (*WordbanksOnline*)

(14)   [The closest any of them came to admitting it] was at one place where the personnel person told me that he'd love to hire me, but he

couldn't.   (Royko (1990))

The sentence in (12) has a meaning such that "Miles had been searching a job for three weeks and what seemed to be the best job for him had been as a kitchen helper in a third-rate, crowded Italian restaurant." As is evident from this interpretation, the head in the bracketed clause in (12) is some kind of job represented by *the closest* but will never be the human represented by *Miles*. The same type of interpretation applies to (13) and (14), as well. Thus I call the bracketed clauses in (12)–(14) HERCs.

[C]   The head of HIRC is an indefinite NP.

As the grammatical judgements in (15) show, the head of HIRC must be an indefinite NP.

(15)   The closest {anyone / ?someone / ?a man / *the man / *John} came to him was the man who leaned over.

This qualification stands in sharp contrast with that in the case of HERCs, because in HERCs, the NP that follows [*the* + Superlative] can be a definite NP *Miles* as in (12), as well as an indefinite NP *anyone* as in (13) and (14). Related to this characteristic seems to be the indefiniteness restriction for the HIRCs in Lakhota, one of the Dakotan dialects spoken by the Sioux Indians in North America. Williamson (1987: 169) states that "the internal head [= the head of HIRC in Lakhota—K.N.] must be indefinite." From the viewpoint of Universal Grammar, this kind of indefiniteness restriction is of profound interest, because English and Lakhota are never said to be related to each other in any typological and historical perspective. For all the unrelatedness between the two languages, they have in common the indefiniteness restriction on HIRCs, which we could argue is one of the linguistic universals.

[D]   Comparison and contrast between HIRC and Free Relative Clause (FRC)

There are two types of FRCs: one is indefinite FRC with *-ever* and the other is definite FRC without.[4] The distribution of HIRCs is the same as that

---

[4] This terminology is after Baker (1989). In Baker's (1995) terminology, however, while the clause headed by *what* is called definite FRC, the one headed by *whatever* is called conditional FRC.

58   *A Dynamic Study of Some Derivative Processes in English Grammar*

of indefinite FRCs in what Nakau (1977) calls "kakuteiteki (referentially fixed)" context. See below:

(16) Terry must have read {*whatever/what} Leah wrote, namely an article on penguins.   (Baker (1989: 173))

(17) {*Whatever/What} John bought, which cost a lot, was broken two days later.   (Cf. Akmajian (1979: 81))

(18) *The closest anyone came to him, namely John Smith, was the man who leaned over.

(19) *The closest anyone came to him, who was wearing a hat, was the man who leaned over.

In the "referentially fixed" context as seen above, HIRC and indefinite FRC do not have an appositive phrase nor a non-restrictive relative clause following them. On the other hand, definite FRC allows either of them after it.

Now it is clear that HIRCs and indefinite FRCs have a formal property in common: in both of them, their heads are indefinite NPs.

[E]   The head in a relative clause is quantified.

Consider the following commonplace HERC:

(20) John read [the book$_i$ [which (WH)$_i$ [Mary bought t$_i$ for him]]]

In the structure of (20), the head in the relative clause is in the form of trace that is bound by the quantifier WH, this binding being guaranteed by co-indexing. That the trace is bound by the quantifier means that the trace is quantified. In other words, the head noun in the relative clause is quantified. Now observe the HIRCs in (9)–(11), relevant portions of which are repeated below:

(9)   [The closest <u>anyone</u> came to him] was the man who leaned over.

(10) [The closest <u>anyone</u> has come] is the ubiquitous Bruce Lindsey.

(11) Michael Heseltine was [the nearest <u>any</u> of them got to the heart of Europe].

The head nouns in these HIRCs are of the form *anyone* or *any*. It is customary in predicate logic to take *any* as a realization of (universal) quantifier. So, we say, in this case, too, that the head in the relative clause is quantified. Thus, whatever type the relative clause may be, the head in the relative clause is quantified.

[F] Finite subordinate clauses are headed by clause introducers (CIs).

What typically functions as a CI in English is a syntactic category called subordinate conjunction, but that is not all that count as CIs. In English, there are a variety of finite subordinate clauses. English finite subordinate clauses include embedded declaratives, indirect questions, indirect exclamations, and HERCs, among others. Below is a short list of the types of finite subordinate clauses and their respective CIs:

(21) a. Subordinate declaratives are headed by *that* or Ø.
    (I think {that / Ø} John is a genius.)
  b. Indirect questions are headed by interrogative WHs.
    (I don't know who you're going to see.
    / I don't know where you met John.)
  c. Indirect exclamations are headed by exclamatory WHs.
    (John told us how beautiful the sunset was.)
  d. HERCs are headed by relative WHs, *that*, or Ø.
    (John read the book {which / that / Ø} Mary bought for him.)

In addition to such ordinary "conjunctions" as *that* and Ø in (21a), we have other CIs that are WH "pronouns" or WH "adverbs" as in (21b–d). Furthermore, there are still other syntactic categories than those in (21) that do function as CIs. Observe the following:

(22) [Immediately John entered the room], Mary burst into tears.

(23) We should have gotten off the plane [the second we overheard the pilot say he's an ex-Blue Angel]. (McPherson (1997))

(24) [The more you get], the more you want.

(25) The state's economy is [the worst it has been in recent history]. (Schwirtz (1992))

(26) [The best the computer can do to improve] is accept software refinements from human programmers. (Gates (1996))

(27) [The closest Miles had been to a job in three weeks of searching] had been as a kitchen helper in a third-rate, crowded Italian restaurant. (= (12))

In (22), an adverb *immediately* functions as a CI, and in (23), the NP *the second* bears the function of CI. In (24), [*the* + Comparative] functions as a CI, while in (25)–(27) [*the* + Superlative] acts as a CI. So, it is noteworthy that CI comprises a whole variety of different syntactic categories.

One thing is concluded from the above facts and observations: for all their syntactic categorial differences, it is clear that conjunctions, WH pronouns, WH adverbs, certain NPs, comparatives and superlatives all conspire to assume one specific syntactic function, i.e. to lead a finite subordinate clause. As Kisseberth (1970) once pointed to the conspiracy in phonology, so we could also speak of the conspiracy in syntax, leading to a syntactico-functional category CI.[5]

Now, HIRCs are finite subordinate clauses, so their observance of the principle of CI conspiracy is expected to be borne out, and it turns out to be the case as seen in (9)–(11), where [*the* + Superlative] introduces the finite subordinate clauses.

[G] Double analysis is possible where there is a structure that bridges HERCs and HIRCs.

We noted previously that there is a family resemblance between HIRCs and the HERC structures in (12)–(14). But there is a crucial difference between the two constructions, the difference in the interpretation of the head. In one case, the head is *anyone* or *any*, but in the other, the head is [*the* + Superlative]. Though it may seem that the two constructions are distinctly different from each other, there is a case where we have a HERC that allows for a head-internal interpretation. Observe the sentence in (28):

(28) [The nearest any western fighting technique has come to the eastern martial arts], is in the French art of "la Savate." *(BNC)*

In (28) the head of the bracketed clause can be interpreted as either *the nearest* or *any western fighting technique*. Here, it is very important to note that

---

[5] For other cases of syntactic conspiracy, see Kajita (1974).

Chapter 6 The Genesis of English Head-Internal Relative Clauses 61

in either case, the meaning of the entire sentence is virtually the same. The sentence of (28) is, as it were, a bridge construction that relates HERC and HIRC. Thus the bridge construction is a construction that has double analysis available.

So far in this section, we observed a number of syntactic features that characterize HIRCs.

6.3.2. Semantics of HERC and HIRC

Before we look into the structure and interpretation of (28), repeated here below, a re-examination of the meanings of HERC and HIRC is in order.

(28) [The nearest any western fighting technique has come to the eastern martial arts], is in the French art of "la Savate."

First, consider the meaning of (12) as shown below in (29):

(29) The meaning of (12):
   (12) [The closest Miles had been to a job in three weeks of search-ing] had been as a kitchen helper in a third-rate, crowded Italian restaurant.

   Miles → → → → → (the closest point)
   [~ A JOB]————————————————+————————————[A JOB]
                    (a kitchen helper)

The scale in (29) shows a gradience of job-likeness, where the right extreme indicates a full-time job, perhaps honorable and well-paid, and the left extreme the state of having no job at all. The illustration means that when Miles had come closest to a full-time job, he was on the spot marked by "+" on the gradience scale and the job was as a kitchen helper in a third-rate, crowded Italian restaurant. Thus the head of the bracketed clause of (12) means the job on the scale. And the head is represented by *the closest*, which evidently shows that the bracketed clause is HERC.

Next, let us consider the meaning of (9) as shown below in (30):

(30) The meaning of (9):

(9) [The closest anyone came to him] was the man who leaned over.

Person A → → → →
Person B → → → → → →
Person C → → → → → → → →

(Person C was the man who leaned over.)

[*away from* HIM]——————————————————+————[HIM]

The scale in (30) shows a gradience of distance from "him," i.e. HIM. The right extreme of the scale indicates the place where "him" is, and the left extreme the point far away from "him." The illustration means that among those who came close to "him," Person C was the closest to "him," and Person C was the man who leaned over. Thus the head of the bracketed clause of (9) means the entity that moved along the scale and came closest to "him." And the head is represented by *anyone*, which evidently shows that the bracketed clause is HIRC.

Finally, consider the meaning of (28) as shown below in (31):

(31) The meaning of (28):

(28) [The nearest any western fighting technique has come to the eastern martial arts], is in the French art of "la Savate."

Western fighting technique → → → → → → (the nearest point)
[~EMA]——————————————————+————[EMA]

(the French art of "la Savate")

The scale in (31) shows a gradience of eastern-martial-arts-likeness, where the right extreme indicates the typical eastern martial arts [EMA], e.g. karate and judo, and the left extreme the non-eastern martial arts [~EMA]. The illustration means that when some western fighting technique has come nearest to the eastern martial arts, it is on the spot marked by "+" on the gradience scale and the type of the martial arts is in the French art of "la Savate." Thus the head of the bracketed clause of (28) means the type of the martial arts on the scale. And the head is represented by *the nearest*, which evidently shows that the bracketed clause is HERC.

On the other hand, (28) actually allows another interpretation. Observe (32):

Chapter 6   The Genesis of English Head-Internal Relative Clauses   63

(32)   The meaning of (28):
　　　　(28) [The nearest any western fighting technique has come to the
　　　　　　 eastern martial arts], is in the French art of "la Savate."
　　Western fighting technique A → → →
　　Western fighting technique B → → → → →
　　Western fighting technique C → → → → → → → (the nearest point)
　　[~EMA]————————————————————————————+——[EMA]
　　　　　　　　　　　　　　　　　　　　　　(the French art of "la Savate")

The illustration in (32) means that among those western fighting techniques that have come near to the eastern martial arts, western fighting technique C is the nearest to it, and western fighting technique C is in the French art of "la Savate." Thus the head of the bracketed clause of (28) means the entity that moves along the scale and comes nearest to the eastern martial atrs. And the head is represented by *any western fighting technique*, which evidently shows that the bracketed clause is HIRC. Note here that the head-external interpretation illustrated in (31) and the head-internal interpretation illustrated in (32) have virtually the same meaning.

　　Now consider the import that the construction (28) bears on our analysis. The construction (28) is a HERC and allows for a head-internal interpretation, which means that double analysis is available with respect to the construction (28). In this sense, the construction (28) is a bridge construction that makes it possible for us to have an access both to HERC and HIRC.

6.4.　The Genesis of HIRC

　　The main concern of this section is to explore the process through which English HIRCs are made possible. We propose the following three stages that are vital to the reinterpretation of the heads in the relative clauses.

(33)   The Genesis of English HIRCs
　　　　Stage 1: HERC as the base structure
　　　　Stage 2: Existence of a bridge construction: HERC with double anal-
　　　　　　　　 ysis available
　　　　Stage 3: Genuine HIRC made possible

At Stage 1, we have HERCs in the form of [[*the* + Superlative] + NP + VP], such as those in (12)–(14), as repeated below:

(12) [The closest Miles had been to a job in three weeks of searching] had been as a kitchen helper in a third-rate, crowded Italian restaurant.

(13) The Monte Carlo Challenge is [the closest anyone gets these days to recapturing the magic of the 1950s and 1960s] when it was regarded as one of the supreme tests of car and driver.

(14) [The closest any of them came to admitting it] was at one place where the personnel person told me that he'd love to hire me, but he couldn't.

These HERCs distinctly have head-external interpretations such that the head is the phrase [*the* + Superlative], and no head-internal interpretation is allowable in these instances. We regard this construction as the base structure.

At Stage 2, we have a HERC in the form of the base structure, but this HERC allows for a head-internal interpretation. The very structure at this stage is (28), which is repeated below:

(28) [The nearest any western fighting technique has come to the eastern martial arts], is in the French art of "la Savate."

In (28), the bracketed clause has the head-external interpretation, and at the same time it gives way to the head-internal interpretation as well, as we observed in the last sections §§6.3.1–2, specifically regarding the feature [G]. Thus, Stage 2 is the stage when we have a bridge construction like (28), and this construction allows for double analysis.

Once the breakthrough of double analysis has been made possible at Stage 2, we could expect the existence of genuine HIRCs, and this is in fact the case at Stage 3. In genuine HIRCs as in (9)–(11), which I repeat below, the only interpretation possible is the head-internal interpretation.

(9) [The closest anyone came to him] was the man who leaned over.

(10) [The closest anyone has come] is the ubiquitous Bruce Lindsey.

(11) Michael Heseltine was [the nearest any of them got to the heart of Europe].

Chapter 6 The Genesis of English Head-Internal Relative Clauses   65

As outlined above, the genesis of HIRCs is the outcome of the step-by-step process that goes from Stage 1 through Stage 3. In other words, HIRCs are impossible up to Stage 1, and they are made possible only after Stage 2. From a theoretical point of view, this type of analysis can be termed as "process-oriented," which is the notion Kajita (1997, 2002) characterizes as opposed to "output-oriented." We will turn to a theoretical discussion in §6.8.

6.5. The Structure of the English HIRCs

Let us now consider how English HIRCs are derived and what their structures are like. The structure that underlies such a HIRC as (9) is (34):

(34) [NP [S' [CI   ] [S [Quantified Head NP anyone] came (the) closest to him]]] was the man who leaned over.

This underlying structure is converted to (35) by moving the phrase *the closest* to the clause-initial position, this position being reserved for the clause introducer (CI) in a finite subordinate clause.

(35) [NP [S' [CI the closest] [S [Quantified Head NP anyone] came to him]]] was the man who leaned over.

The movement of *the closest* is motivated by the two independent grammatical considerations. One is the principle of CI conspiracy mentioned in the previous section §6.3.1 regarding the feature [F]. According to this principle, finite subordinate clauses have a CI and a variety of phrases, one being of the form [*the* + Superlative], in particular, conspire to assume a CI function. The other motivation that activates the movement of *the closest* is a typological tendency such that "postnominal relatives [= relative clauses that follow the nominal head, such as English relatives—K.N.] may be preceded by a morphologically invariant complementizer (Keenan 1985:160)." This tendency forces the phrase *the closest* to precede the finite relative clause, resulting in the movement of *the closest* from the sentence-internal position to the sentence-initial position. Now we have arrived at the structure (35), a surface structure of a HIRC.

Next, let us consider the structural requirements for the HIRC, as well as for the HERC. A typical, commonplace HERC is like (20), which is repeated here:

(20) John read [the book$_i$ [which(WH)$_i$ [Mary bought t$_i$ for him]]]

So it is clearly the case that both HERCs and HIRCs have the same structural requirements as shown in (36) and (37), respectively.

(36) The structural requirements for the English HERCs:
    a. The relative clause is headed by CI.
    b. The head in the relative clause is quantified.

(37) The structural requirements for the English HIRCs:
    a. The relative clause is headed by CI.
    b. The head in the relative clause is quantified.

The very sameness of the structural requirements in these two structures strongly suggests that HIRC is a natural extension from HERC.

6.6. Other Data Explained

If the analysis thus far presented is on the right track, it can accommodate another domain of data that has been regarded as a longstanding puzzle. Observe the following:

(38) ?[Anybody does that] ought to be locked up.

(Quirk et al. (1985: 1250))

(39) *[The table stands in the corner] has a broken leg. (ibid.)

Quirk et al. (1985) seek to explore the condition that permits the deletion of subjective relative pronouns. According to them (Quirk et al. 1985: 1251), the ungrammaticality of (39) is perhaps due to the failure of perception, i.e., sentence processing fails when a reader / hearer encounters *has* in (39). If their account is correct, (38) should be judged as bad as (39). But, as Quirk et al. (1985: 1250) admit, the fact is that (38) is found in very informal speech though it is questionable or doubtful. They only hint at the difference between (38) and (39) such that in (38) "the antecedent is an indefinite pronoun (Quirk et al. 1985: 1250)." But they give no further discussion.

In our analysis, the bracketed portions in (38) and (39) are both HIRCs.

Chapter 6   The Genesis of English Head-Internal Relative Clauses   67

Now, recall the structural requirements in (37). In the case of (38), the head NP *anybody* is quantified, as is evident from the morphological composition of the phrase [*any* + one], and this clause lacks a CI. Here, one requirement is satisfied. Hence "?" In the case of (39), the head NP *the table* is not quantified, and the clause lacks a CI. Neither of the requirements is satisfied. Hence "*." Thus our analysis accommodates quite straightforwardly the data (38) and (39).

Next, consider the example below:

(40) a. [Anyone knowing his whereabouts] should contact the police.

(Huddleston and Pullum (2002: 1188))

b. If anyone knows his whereabouts, he/she should contact the police.

N. Nakazawa (2005: 74) leaves open the problem of how the subject NP of (40a) arrives at a conditional interpretation as in (40b). Apart from this problem, we see a family resemblance in (40a) and (38). In (38), the bracketed clause is a HIRC, while the bracketed portion in (40a) may be a clause or a phrase. According to our analysis, however, the bracketed portion in (40a) is in fact "sentential," but it is nonfinite. Recall that finite subordinate clauses require a CI, but the nonfinites never do so. The head of the bracketed clause in (40a), i.e. *anyone*, is quantified, but the clause itself does not need a CI because of its nonfiniteness. Thus (40a) is perfectly grammatical. Our analysis proceeds straightforwardly in this case, too.

6.7. Possible Counterarguments

It is conceivable to argue against our analysis in such a way that the phrase structure of (9) is not what we presented in (35), but rather should look like the following:[6]

(41) [NP [S [NP The closest anyone] came to him]] was the man who leaned over.

---

[6] I have received this type of counterargument several times. One such occasion was at the 23rd Conference of the English Linguistic Society of Japan held at Kyushu University in November, 2005.

There are a number of defects in the proposed structure of (41). One is that we never have a form "*the closest anyone."

Second, if the structure in (41) is permissible, we immediately encounter the same problem that Quirk et al. (1985) did, regarding the grammaticality diversity among (41), (38) and (39): they are "perfectly OK," "?" and "*," respectively. If we suppose that all three of them are derived simply by way of subject relative pronoun deletion, why is it the case that such a diversity in grammaticality is possible? Quirk et al. (1985) might be tempted to say that the indefiniteness of the subject pronoun would be the key feature that distinguishes "grammatical / questionable" from "ungrammatical." But they will fail to explain the difference between "perfectly OK" in (41) and "?" in (38).

Third, deletion of the subject relative pronouns is a highly restricted phenomenon, as is discussed in Lambrecht (1988), Ukaji (2003) and N. Nakazawa (2006), among others. Subject relative pronoun deletion is only permitted in the following two types of grammatical environments (the antecedents of the deleted subject relative pronouns are underlined):

(42) This is the guy we think is the leading figure of the ring.

One such environment is "NP + [relative pronoun] + NP." When a relative pronoun is in this environment, irrespective of whether it is subjective or objective, it can be deleted. In the case of (42), the sequence "[NP the guy] + [relative pronoun] + [NP we]" qualifies for the deletion of a relative pronoun, which account is responsible for the absence of a relative pronoun in (42). Note incidentally that this environment is also found in the case of (20), where deletion of the objective relative pronoun is possible. But observe (41), where the structure prior to the deletion of a subject relative pronoun looks like "[NP the closest anyone] + [relative pronoun] + [V came]." This sequence does not qualify for the intended deletion, so the proposal for the structure in (41) fails.

The other environment in which subject relative pronoun deletion is permitted is as follows:

(43) a. There was a farmer had a dog.
      b. This is the girl wants to see you.
      c. Here's the boy'll fix it for you.
      d. I have a brother works in Dublin.

Chapter 6   The Genesis of English Head-Internal Relative Clauses   69

  e. I'm the only one knows how to act.
  f. It's Simon did it.   (N. Nakazawa (2006: 71-72))

Phrases before the underlined antecedents in (43) all have such a function as to introduce into the discourse a certain referent that bears new information. In other words, subject relative pronoun deletion is possible only in what might be termed the presentational context. But observe the case of (41). It does not make any sense to say that *the closest anyone* in (41) is a presentational context. So, we argue that (41) is not eligible for subject relative pronoun deletion, and, therefore, that the subject NP of (41) does not have the structure depicted in (41).

 Fourth, if the structure in (41) is tenable, we could not expect any phonological break between "the closest" and "anyone." But the fact is that there is the same type of phonological break between "the closest" and "anyone" in (41), be it perceivable to our ears or not, as there is between "the more" and "you" in (24), between "the worst" and "it" in (25), between "the best" and "the computer" in (26), and between "the closest" and "Miles" in (27). This shows that there is in fact a structural break that we have between a CI and the following subject NP in the case of (41).

 Fifth, the proponents of the analysis presented in (41) must note the fact that the number of genuine HIRCs is quite small, in fact as small as four, including the bridge construction (28). These four instances are all I have found so far in the raw data. If the structure of (41) is a standard type of nominal structure, we would expect a huge number of occurrences of this construction. But this is not the case. The preciously minor status of HIRC can only be explained through a step-by-step "process-oriented" analysis, as given in §6.4.

 For all these reasons given above, the structure of (41) is judged far away from the correct nominal structure.

 We may expect some other form of counterargument such that all the instances in (9)-(11) are in fact ungrammatical structures, which escaped our grammar-conscious eyes and accidentally popped out into the world. If so, how is it possible to explain the grammaticality diversity found in (9)-(11), on the one hand, and (38) and (39), on the other? Our analysis is ready to do the job. In addition, we could accommodate another type of structure, i.e. (40a). Furthermore, the native informants I consulted all agreed that sentences like (9)-(11) are fine, and some gave me additional examples of their own making, some of which are as follows:

(44) a. The closest I was to Princess Diana was at the reception party held during her stay in Japan.

b. The closest any president came to me was George Bush, Sr.

When asked about the construction of (9), an informant I consulted gave me (44a). It should be noted that he is not a linguist but is so kind as to give me (44a) to further illustrate the construction at issue. Notice that (9) is a HIRC and (44a) a HERC, but he thinks that (9) and (44a) are of the same type of construction. His observation endorses the correctness of the "process-oriented" approach to the genesis of HIRCs, in which we assume that HIRCs are possible forms of extension from HERCs. Another informant I consulted, who is a linguist, gave me (44b) as an additional example of HIRC. All these prove the grammatical productivity of English HIRCs for native speakers of English, however unconscious they may be of the rules that produce them. Therefore, the counterargument that (9)–(11) are all ungrammatical does not have any substantial basis.

There is another type of possible counterargument such that (9), for example, should be understood as an instance of inverted construction as in (45):

(45) Handsome was the man who leaned over.

But this argument is also untenable. The reason is as follows. In the inverted construction like (45), *handsome* is not a subject, as is evidenced by the ungrammaticality of the subject-raising constructions in (46):

(46) a. *Handsome seemed to be the man who leaned over.

b. *Handsome was likely to be the man who leaned over.

c. *Handsome is believed to be the man who leaned over.

But *the closest anyone came to him* in (9) is definitely a subject, as is evidenced by the grammaticality of the subject-raising constructions in (47):

(47) a. The closest anyone came to him seemed to be the man who leaned over.

b. The closest anyone came to him was likely to be the man who leaned over.

c. The closest anyone came to him is believed to be the man who leaned over.

Therefore, the construction (9) is not an inverted construction, but rather it is a construction with a HIRC in the subject position.

6.8. Theoretical Issues

In this section, we are concerned with the characterization of our analysis from a theoretical point of view.

First of all, as regards descriptive adequacy, any grammar failing to describe English HIRCs should be judged descriptively inadequate. Our analysis, on the other hand, is, needless to say, descriptively adequate, since one of the objectives of this chapter is to reveal the existence of the English HIRCs, and so we did.

In §6.1, we referred to the theoretical prediction made by Cole (1987) and Kayne (1994) such that English does not have HIRCs. One of the structures they excluded as theoretically impossible is (6a), among others, which is repeated below:

(6) a. $[_{NP} [_{S'} ...NP (lexical)...]]$

Now it is clear that there are English HERCs that have the very structure of (6a). Let us repeat them below:

(12) [The closest Miles had been to a job in three weeks of searching] had been as a kitchen helper in a third-rate, crowded Italian restaurant.

(13) The Monte Carlo Challenge is [the closest anyone gets these days to recapturing the magic of the 1950s and 1960s] when it was regarded as one of the supreme tests of car and driver.

(14) [The closest any of them came to admitting it] was at one place where the personnel person told me that he'd love to hire me, but he couldn't.

We have no idea of how Cole (1987) and Kayne (1994) would analyze the structures in (12)–(14), but certainly *the closest* is both the CI of the clause and the head of the respective subject NPs in (12)–(14).

Another point of interest is that HERCs in (12)–(14) share a family resemblance with the genuine HIRCs, whose basic structure is that of (6a), the latter structure being abandoned by Cole (1987) and Kayne (1994).

Our analysis intending to account for the genesis of English HIRCs has assumed three adjacent successive stages. The process develops this way: Stage 1 is presupposed for Stage 2 to be made possible, and Stage 2 is presupposed for Stage 3 to be made possible. This type of analysis conforms to the general theory format shown in (48):

(48)   If the grammar of a language L at stage i, G(L, i), has property P, then the grammar of the language at the next stage, G(L, i+1), may have property P′.   (Kajita (2002: 161))

Any theory incorporating (48) as one of its components is called a theory of grammatical dynamism, or sometimes a dynamic theory (of grammar), or Grammatical Dynamism for short. Thus, it is argued that our analysis is one possible instantiation of the theory format in (48). Thus English HERCs of the structure (6a) are the prerequisite for the bridge construction (28). The bridge construction (28) is the prerequisite for the genuine HIRCs. Our analysis proposed in this chapter provides a step-by-step treatment of the variety of the relatives that come into our view, some of which Cole (1987) and Kayne (1994) would certainly fail to accommodate, and it moves along the theory format of (48). In this sense, our analysis argues for Grammatical Dynamism.

The English HIRC has a number of construction-particular characteristics. One is that this construction seems to be a very minor construction; in other words, it will find its own place on the periphery of English grammar. Related to this is the fact that the number of observed instances of English HIRCs is so small, as we mentioned in the last section.[7] Another characteris-

---

[7] I consulted such electronic databases as *BNC* and *WordbanksOnline*. I used a variety of superlatives and quantifiers as the key words to search for HIRCs, but nearly every effort was unsuccessful.

Needless to say, HERCs of the form (i) below, where [*the* + Superlative] is the head of the entire NP, are commonly found.

(i)   [NP [S′ [*the* + Superlative] + [*any* ...] + VP]]]

They include examples of (12), (13) and (14) in §6.3.1. Some other examples of the form (i) are as follows:

(ii)   [NP The closest anyone can get to a dream vacation] lies just around 400 miles north of Tampa.   (Katie Toot, *Tampa Bay Metro Magazine* 2011, p. 1)

Chapter 6   The Genesis of English Head-Internal Relative Clauses   73

tic is that this construction seems to have emerged by way of item-specific extension. Superlatives used in the genuine HIRCs are confined to *closest* and
nearest, and quantifiers used to quantify the head in the relative clause are, in
reality, confined only to *any*. But item-specific extension itself is not uncom-
mon, for children in the earlier stages of language acquisition would say,
"Mommy come!" but would never say, "*Linguist come!" The Noun *linguist*
is one of the least probable words for them. This is because it seems reasonable to suppose that children would acquire the syntactic category of Noun
through an item-specific process, i.e. first, the family members' names, kinship
terms, toys and cartoon characters, and so on, and finally such abstract nouns
as *realism, democracy, underdevelopment.* If this process of acquiring Nouns
is for the most part correct, the item *linguist* would never emerge in the early
stages of acquisition because this Noun has nothing to do with children's daily
concerns and activities. Thus the absence of "*Linguist come!" in the earlier
stages of acquisition can be explained in terms of the item-specific extension
in the acquisition of Nouns. As the rarity of the Noun *linguist* in childhood is

---

(iii)   And a number of people voiced their support during the half-hour question-and-
answer period. [NP The closest anyone came to criticism] occurred when Las Ve-
gas musician and artist Ginger Bruner, who has longstanding ties to the Huntridge
and surrounding neighborhood, asked why Huntridge Revival was going forward
as a for-profit venture. Her question sparked a small wave of applause; the question of for-profit versus noprofit has divided some of those who want to see the
theater resurrected.
(Launce Rake, "Opponents of Huntridge Revival have plenty to say on Facebook
but skip community meeting," (lasvegascitylife.com/sections/news/opponents-hunt-
ridge-revival-have-plenty-say-facebook-skip-community-meeting.html)

(iv)   Nevertheless, Rome insists water baptism is absolutely essential for salvation, it
supposedly being the only way to get rid of original sin staining the soul. But
where on earth did this so-called original sin come from? We know that Adam
and Eve committed the first human sin, and that all who are descendents of theirs
have inherited the inclination to do evil. But nowhere in the Word of God can be
found even one passage saying we have Adam's sin on our soul at the moment we
are born. [NP The nearest anyone can get to that belief] is found in two Psalms of
David: 1) *"Behold, I was shapen in iniquity; and in sin did my mother conceive
me."* (Psa 5 1:5) And, 2) *"The wicked are estranged from the womb: they go
astray as soon as they be born, speaking lies."* (Psa 58:3) In the first cited verse,
the sin was not David's but his parent's, and in the second, the "wicked" referred
to are "estranged" as soon as they are born, but not while in the womb. [Italics
original.]   (Schroeder (2004: 162–163))

I am indebted to Masaaki Fuji for the examples (ii)–(iv).

due to item-specific extension, so the characteristic regarding both the small variety of the superlatives and the de facto only one instance of the quantifier *any* in HIRCs is due to the same principle. All of these construction-particular characteristics will fit so well in the dynamic view of grammatical extension, outlined in (48).

We believe that our analysis describes the process leading to the genesis of English HIRCs in the way it really is: no overgeneration is expected, nor is any undergeneration observed. Thus it is claimed that the theory on which our analysis is based is adequately rich and properly constrained.

Appendix

What follows is an appendix to Chapter 6. Its title is "The Intensional Qualification of Quantification." Chapter 6 dealt with the issue of how English HIRCs are made possible in the grammar of English referring to the general schema of construction extension, i.e. Grammatical Dynamism. In this chapter, notions such as "to quantify," "quantification," and "quantified NPs" played a significantly important role in the analysis of English HIRCs. But what is the notion "quantification"? The appendix below is an attempt to answer this question.

Appendix to Chapter 6:
The Intensional Qualification of Quantification

6a.1. Introduction

This appendix explores the possibility of defining Quantification from the intensional point of view and discusses some of its empirical consequences.[8]

6a.2. Three Types of Definition

There are three types of definition as shown in (1) below:

(1) a. Intensional definition

---

[8] This appendix is a slightly revised version of Nakazawa (2002b).

Chapter 6   The Genesis of English Head-Internal Relative Clauses   75

    b. Extensional definition

    c. No way

Let us illustrate how each type is related to the actual manner of defining things.

    When you are confronted with the question (2a), you will answer like (2b). This is the definition by way of intension.

(2) a. What is the even number?

     b. It is a number that is "divisible by two without a remainder."

(COD s.v. *even*)

Intensional definition means the characterization of things in terms of the features or qualities that the things in question possess.

    When you are confronted with the question (3a), you will answer like (3b). This is the definition by way of extension.

(3) a. What is the normal solar spectrum?

     b. Consult *Webster*[3] and go to the inserted leaf between the pages 448 and 449. You will know (or see) what it is like.

Extensional definition is the definition in terms of realia, without any verbal explication.

    When you are confronted with the question (4a), you have no way to answer it but to simply paraphrase the notion asked in a number of ways, for example, using such terms as *spot, place, mark,* and *dot,* as in (4c):

(4) a. What is 'point' in Euclidean geometry?

     b. (No way to define it)

     c. It is "a particular spot or place; or a very small dot or mark on a surface."

(COD s.v. *point*)

Therefore, the third type of definition is, in fact, not a definition. In this case, the notions asked are primitives. Primitives are, by definition, non-defined notions.

6a.3.   Definition of Quantification

    Our primary concern in this section is (5):

(5) What is Quantification?

It seems that in the literature of linguistics, Quantification is, most of the times, defined in the manner of (1b).[9] But I assume that Quantification can be, and should be, defined in the following way:

(6) Quantification is predication of one and the same item x that appears in more than one clause.

The notion "to quantify" can be defined like below accordingly:

(7) When there are clauses of the forms $(_A...x...)$, $(_B... x...)$, and so on, to quantify x is to predicate the one and the same x in each of these clauses.

Though these two definitions are gross approximations, they are clearly the definitions in the manner of (1a).[10] Furthermore, they have certain empirical

---

[9] To see this, I can cite passages from a number of references.

(i) [Referring to "For every x, x is a miser"]
The phrase 'for every x' is called a *universal quantifier.* (Suppes (1957: 48))

(ii) The prefixes '$(\exists x)$', '$(\exists y)$', etc. are called *quantifiers;* and the construction of statements with their help is called quantification. Also a statement so formed will be called a quantification. (Quine (1965: 75))

(iii) The *universal quantifier,* denoted by $\forall$, corresponds to phrases such as 'for each,' 'for all,' 'for every,' and 'for any.' The *existential quantifier,* denoted by $\exists$, has as its English counterparts 'there exists,' 'for some,' 'there is at least one,' etc. Wherever a quantifier occurs, it is associated with some variable, and we shall represent this in our notation by enclosing the symbols for the quantifier and its associated variable in parentheses; thus, $(\forall x),(\exists y)$. The universal and existential quantifications of the propositional function $M(x)$ are written as in (3–4) and (3–5), respectively:
(3–4) $(\forall x)\ M(x)$
(3–5) $(\exists x)\ M(x)$ (Wall (1972: 53))

(iv) A quantifier is a word or expression that specifies which or how many of some kind of things have some property, as here, where *All/Most crooks tell lies* says which crooks or how many crooks have the property of telling lies.
(McCawley (1993: 23))

There are many other authors and passages of this sort: they try to define Quantification basically in the manner of (1b). But I understand that they are not necessarily rigorously particular about the definition of the notion in question, so I will not go into this issue any further.

[10] (6) and (7) are of my own thinking. I learned independently that there are similar characterizations of Quantification by some philosopher-logicians. Roughly speaking, a quantifier is defined as a functor that assigns a relation among domains. Cf. Mostowski

Chapter 6   The Genesis of English Head-Internal Relative Clauses   77

consequences and, in some cases, some advantages over the old definitions through which many linguists have manipulated a number of syntactic and semantic analyses.

6a.4.   Consequences of Intensional Definition of Quantification

It has been generally assumed that Quantification is operative both in the interpretation of quantity phrases, e.g. phrases with *all*, *some*, *ten*, *many*, and *a*, and in the interpretation of WH phrases. And the latter has two major subcases, i.e. Relative WH phrases and Interrogative WH phrases.

Our first advantage due to the employment of (6) and (7) is such that the commonality between quantity phrases and WH phrases can be captured through our definition of Quantification. Consider the following cases:

(8) a.   Joe has a girlfriend.
   b.   (There is x) [x = a girlfriend]
   c.   (Joe has x)

(9) a.   Joe ate the apple that / which Sue bought.
   b.   (Joe ate x) [x = an apple]
   c.   (Sue bought x)

(10) a.   What did Joe eat?
    b.   (I WANT TO KNOW THE IDENTITY OF x)
    c.   (Joe ate x)

(8a) involves in it a quantity phrase, and (9a) and (10a) involve WH phrases in them. Interpretation of (8a) comprises a process of predication of x that appears both in (8b) and in (8c). Precisely in the same way, interpretation of (9a) comprises a process of predication of x that appears both in (9b) and in (9c). And this statement applies equally to the case of (10). Therefore, since we have adopted the definitions of (6) and (7), we capture the similarity or, we should say, the identity of the manner of interpretation in both cases of quantity phrases and WH phrases.

On the other hand, suppose that we do not adopt (6) and (7) and simply

---

(1957) and Lindström (1966). I believe that formulations of the forms (6) and (7) are more congenial to linguists and linguistics than the ones the aforementioned philosopher-logicians have developed.

78   A Dynamic Study of Some Derivative Processes in English Grammar

say, for example, that the indefinite article *a* is a quantifier and a relative pronoun is a quantifier in the interpretation of the sentences those expressions are embedded in. In other words, suppose that we simply list quantifiers and do not give them any intensional characterization at all. Then we can say that this is only a linguists' stipulation and does not answer the question of why quantity phrases and WH phrases behave in the same manner, with respect to the interpretation of sentences in which these quantity phrases and WH phrases are predicated of. So there is no other way than to conclude that the identical process of interpretation in the cases of (8), (9), and (10) is a mere coincidence. There is no explanation made possible here in these cases as to the striking identity of the manner of interpretation of sentences with all these different types of words, i.e. *a*, *that/which* and *what*: they are an article, a relative pronoun and an interrogative pronoun, respectively. So the definition of Quantification only by way of enumerating quantifiers, in the manner of (1b), is not adequate for the analysis of these cases.

As a second consequence of our adoption of the definitions (6) and (7), we may think of the following cases.[11]

Recall that in (6) and (7) we have simply said that we predicate of an item x and we quantify an item x, respectively. We do not say that we predicate of an 'argument' nor do we say that we quantify an 'argument.' This is mainly because there are sentences with relative clauses in which non-arguments are relativized. Observe the cases below:

(11)   Joe ate the apple that Sue bought. (= (9a))

(12)   Joe left the room where Sue was sleeping.

(13)   Joe was pleased with the headway that Sue made.

In (11), the argument is relativized, and in (12) what is relativized is the locative adjunct, a non-argument. In (13), the non-argument, an idiom chunk in this case, is relativized. So it is now clear that Quantification is not restricted to arguments. Non-arguments can be quantified and relativized. And I will

---

[11] It may be that technically speaking, this consequence might have resulted directly from the phrasing of the syntactic definition of relativization, but the intensional nature of Quantification makes it possible to accommodate both argument and non-argument cases of relativization.

Chapter 6   The Genesis of English Head-Internal Relative Clauses   79

point out another case of the relativization of non-arguments, namely the relativization of superlatives.   But before we go to the cases of the relativization of non-argument superlatives, let us look at the cases of the relativization of argument superlatives.

(14) a.   Thus, [the most Gorbachev can probably expect] is technical help on privatization along with limited private investment in selected projects.   (Charles Lane and Carroll Bogert, "To Market, to Market," *NW* July 22, 1991)

   b.   Charles: "Just a moment.   I'd like to settle the matter of that twit of a major with whom Diana had a merry roll in the hay."

       Diana: "We did not have a roll in the hay.   You know very well that I dislike hay and that it makes me sniffle and does ghastly things to my skin."

       Charles: "Well, I don't really care where you had your roll. Such details bore me.   But [the least you could have done] was have a roll in the whatever with a decent chap who wouldn't dash off to write a bloody book about it.   My word, if Henry the Eighth were your husband, he would have had you and that major drawn and quartered." (Mike Royko, "Notes from a Right Royal Counseling Session," JT October 30, 1994)

The sentences with relatives at stake in (14a) and (14b) have, at a certain stage of semantic interpretation, the structures shown in (15a, b) and (16a, b), respectively:

(15) a.   (*x* is technical help on privatization along with limited private investment in selected projects)

   b.   (Gorbachev can probably expect *x*)

(16) a.   (*x* was (to) have a roll in the whatever with a decent chap who wouldn't dash off to write a bloody book about it)

   b.   (you could have done *x*)

These are the cases of the relativization of argument superlatives.   Now let us observe the cases of the relativization of non-argument superlatives.

(17) a.   The state's economy is [the worst it has been in recent history].
                   (Mira Schwirtz, "Free Agreement," *DC* January 29, 1992)

80   *A Dynamic Study of Some Derivative Processes in English Grammar*

b. It is our impression that there are very few *pure syntactic con-structions*, that is, constructions which have *no* specific semantic or pragmatic functions associated with them and which mention no specific lexical items. [The closest we can come to that] is the *subject-predicate* construction of English. [Italics are original authors'.]   (Charles J. Fillmore and Paul Kay 1987:13)

c. Since then—and it's been almost three years—she's been through one interview after another, all of them ending with something like: "Thank you, very impressive, but ..." [...] [The closest any of them came to admitting it] was at one place where the personnel person told me that he'd love to hire me, but he couldn't. (Mike Royko, "Age is no asset in U.S. job market," *JT* August 3, 1990)

d. Deep Blue could have prevailed in the recent match had Kasparov not changed his style of play after his initial loss. That the chess champ was able so quickly to identify the computer's weakness and adapt his competitive strategy is testimony to human intellect. [The best the computer can do to improve] is accept software refinements from human programmers. (Bill Gates, "Computer will be Chess Champ, but so What?" *JT* March 18, 1996)

The sentences with relatives at issue in (17a–d) have, at a certain stage of semantic interpretation, the following structures (18a, b), (19a, b), (20a, b) and (21a, b), respectively:

(18) a. (the state's economy is *x*)
     b. (it [= the state's economy] has been *x* in recent history)

(19) a. (*x* is the *subject-predicate* construction of English)
     b. (we can come *x* to that)

(20) a. (*x* was at one place where the personnel person told me that he'd love to hire me, but he couldn't)
     b. (any of them came *x* to admitting it)

(21) a. (*x* is accept software refinements from human programmers)

Chapter 6   The Genesis of English Head-Internal Relative Clauses   81

b. (the computer can do x to improve)[12]

These are the cases of the relativization of non-argument superlatives. Observe the b-structures above. This is one of the consequences derived from adopting the definitions of (6) and (7).

A third empirical consequence of adopting (6) and (7) constitutes an advantage over the adoption of old extensional definitions. It has been assumed in the literature that relativization involves the syntactic process shown below. For the sake of exposition, we will confine ourselves to the case of relativization of NPs, and the structures that are of little importance to the present discussion are simplified.

(22) a.   [... [$_{NP}$ NP$_i$ [$_S$ ... NP$_i$ ...]] ...]
      b.   [... [$_{NP}$ NP$_i$ [WH$_i$ [$_S$ ... t$_i$ ...]]] ...]

In order to form a relative clause, the structure (22a) should be converted to the structure (22b). What is assumed in this process, tacitly or otherwise in the literature, is that we have in fact two different components in the process of relativization: if we call the NP to be relativized a 'Coref NP',[13] then the Coref NP should be both WH-quantified and moved to the initial position of the clause in which it is embedded. This general assumption applies, it seems, to every case of relativiation that has so far been observed, documented, and analyzed in the grammar of English. But observe the definitions of (6) and (7) closely. They dictate only the quantification of an NP, the Coref NP in this case, but never dictate the syntactic movement of that NP. So these definitions will leave the case possible such that the Coref NP is quantified but not moved. And this is in fact the case. Contrary to the common linguistic belief that there is no head-internal relative clause in English, I have argued for the existence of English head-internal relative clauses, in which the Coref NP is quantified but stays where it was (cf. Nakazawa 1991, 1999b, and chapter 6 of this thesis). Observe below:

---

[12] It might be that (21) could be a case of the relativization of the argument in that x could be paraphrased as *the best thing*. But I assum that x is an adverb in (21b).

[13] 'Coref NP' is intended to mean the NP to be relativized under the coreferential condition such that the antecedent NP and the NP to be relativized should have the same referential indices.

82   *A Dynamic Study of Some Derivative Processes in English Grammar*

(23) a.   A friend of mine once passed out from heat on a downtown street, falling into the gutter. [The closest <u>anyone</u> came to him] was the man who leaned over, just as my friend was coming to, and said: "Hey, you're blocking my car." (Mike Royko, "Some Good Reasons to Keep Walking," *CT* October 1, 1987; "Woman Gives Aid and Gets AIDS?" *JT* October 30, 1987)[14]

   b.   Mrs. Clinton did not manage to utter the magic words, "not true," and neither, really, has anyone else. [The closest <u>anyone</u> has come] is the ubiquitous Bruce Lindsey, who, rather early in the breaking scandal, was asked directly by the Associated Press whether Mr. Clinton denied having troopers assist any affairs. "Yes, he has," Mr. Lindsey responded. (Editorial in *WT* December 22, 1993; Reprinted in *Sekai Nippou* December 30, 1993)[15]

The sentences with head-internal relatives in (23a) and (23b) have, at a certain stage of semantic interpretation, the following structures, respectively:

(24) a.   (x was the man who leaned over, just as my friend was coming to, and said: "Hey, you're blocking my car")

   b.   (x came (the) closest to him)

(25) a.   (x is the ubiquitous Bruce Lindsey, …)

   b.   (x has come (the) closest)

The striking features of our head-internal relatives are such that the Coref NP is quantified but not moved to the clause-initial position and that the Coref NP is quantified but not WH-quantified. In our head-internal relatives, what is moved to the clause-initial position is the superlative, i.e. *the closest* in the above examples. Now recall the superlatives in the examples of (14) and (17). The former are the instances of the relativization of arguments, and the latter the instances of the relativization of non-arguments. And most importantly, the superlatives in (14), (17), and (23) all share the conspiracy relation such that they function as a clause introducer for the following clauses.[16] The

---

[14] The same column appeared under the different titles.

[15] I am indebted to Takao Ito, who pointed out (23b) to me.

[16] The notion 'clause introducer' has a theoretical status (not just a hocus-pocus entity) and thus prevails in other areas of description in the grammar of English. See, for example, Nakazawa (2000b), which takes advantage of this notion and intends to describe and ana-

Chapter 6   The Genesis of English Head-Internal Relative Clauses   83

second striking feature of the Coref NP in head-internal relatives is related to Quantification: it is quantified but not WH-quantified. This is the natural consequence of the definitions of (6) and (7), because Quantification is by no means restricted to the cases of WH phrases, but applicable to the cases of quantity phrases. This is the most advantageous point of the analysis that adopts the intensional definition of Quantification.

Now let us summarize the argument of the last paragraph from a different point of view. In describing and analyzing English relative clauses, suppose we have two competing grammars, G1 and G2. Suppose further that G1 employs an extensional definition of Quantification and that G2 employs an intensional definition of Quantification. Part of the description of G1 and G2 will be like those below, respectively:

(26) Part of G1 Description
    a. Coref NP is WH-quantified
    b. WH-phrase moves to the clause-initial position

(27) Part of G2 Description
    a. Coref NP is quantified
    b. WH-phrase moves to the clause-initial position

It should be clear that G1 can handle the typical cases of relatives, such as those in (9a) but cannot the head-internal relatives, as in (23). On the other hand, G2 can naturally accommodate both the typical relatives in (9a) and the head-internal relatives in (23). In G2, if the Coref NP is WH-quantified, that phrase goes to the clause-initial position, as dictated by (27b), as in (9a). And also in G2, if the Coref NP is quantified by the quantity phrase, e.g. *any*, it does not move to the clause-initial position as exemplified in (23). This is because the phrases quantified by quantity phrases do not move to the clause-initial position in syntax. See below:

(28) a. I don't see anyone there.
    b. *Anyone I don't see there. (Intended to mean (28a))

---

lyze the behavior of English adverbial NPs. See also Nakazawa (1999b, 2007b).

(29) a. Do you have any question?
b. *Any question do you have?

Now suppose G1 theorists had encountered English head-internal relative clauses like those in (23) and got encouraged to revise their grammar G1 to accommodate these cases. Their revision would take the form of the following:

(30) Part of the Revised G1 Description
a. Coref NP is either WH-quantified or quantity phrase-quantified
b. WH-phrase moves to the clause-initial position

The grammar of (30) is descriptively adequate, but it has a serious defect. It fails to answer the questions of why WH-quantification and quantity phrase-quantification are simply enumerated in (30a), and why only these and not the other. In G2 framework, there is never the type of problem that there is in G1 framework.

6a.5. Summary and Residuals

We have explored the possibility of intensional qualification of Quantification. This type of definition has proved to have a number of empirical consequences and advantages: we can capture the parallel structure in the interpretation of quantity phrases and WH-phrases; we can look for the measures to take to accommodate English head-internal relative clauses.

If the arguments made so far are basically correct, we may have a new insight into the notions of Quantification and Predication. Quantification is a notion that is defined derivatively. But what is Predication? It may be that the very nature of Predication cannot be defined but it is only a primitive. This is a residual problem.

Another residual is the ontology of the processes that govern more than one clause at a time. Why and how do humans come to manipulate notions at a time that belong to more than one independent clause, rather than to speak out clauses sequentially? But this issue goes far beyond the scope of this appendix.

Chapter 7

Water Finds Its Level: Derivatives Find General Rules

7.1. Introduction

Linguists would say that Language is rule-governed.[1] But there are exceptions and exceptions. Some are total pure exceptions that have no regularity in them at all. But others are prone to regularities. As for the former cases, see for example the expressions in (1):

(1) a. *went* (past tense form of *go*)
    b. Away with you!
    c. kingdom come

In (1a), you cannot predict the regular past tense form of *go*, but only have to remember the entire form *went*. Of all the senses and uses of the preposition *with*, the one exemplified in (1b) is one of the most idiosyncratic patterns of usage. *With* in this sentence has no comitative sense, but only governs the following NP that is interpreted as Actor or Theme.[2] And (1c) has survived the metaphorical process of syntactic and semantic distortions and has ended up as what you may call an idiom. Thus (1a–c) are exceptional expressions,

---

[1] This chapter is a slightly revised version of Nakazawa (2001a).
[2] But see chapter 8 for an attempt to analyze this construction.

86   *A Dynamic Study of Some Derivative Processes in English Grammar*

each with some form of irregularity in it.

And as for the latter cases, where exceptions more or less behave regularly, it is this topic to which the following pages are devoted. This chapter is an attempt to shed light on a variety of exceptional linguistic phenomena that have something in common but that have so far, in my view, received little attention and thus have yet to see a systematic treatment.

Linguists have long sought regularities in the specific fields of linguistic investigation: phonologists have sought phonological regularities, semanticists semantic regularities, and syntacticians syntactic regularities. And, by the same token, cognitivists have been working on the cognitive regularities of human behavior, linguistic activities being a part of it.

In the following, we will observe certain types of linguistic phenomena, the analyses of which are purported to be made in a number of grammatical components, i.e. phonology, lexicon / morphology and syntax. But the generalizations induced from the analyses of these phenomena reveal that we should not pertain to the division of the grammatical components in order to understand the nature of such regularities as found in those irregularities that we observe in the following sections. Instead, it will be shown, we should ascribe the nature of this type of regularities to our mental faculty in general. We will return to this topic in the last section of this chapter, i.e. §7.6.

7.2. Exceptions and Regularities in Phonology

7.2.1. Primary Stress Placement

English has a well-established rule of assigning the primary stress to the penultimate syllable in the adjectives that have an *-ic* ending. Hereafter I will mention only the primary stress and disregard the secondary, tertiary and other stresses. The phonetic facts are based on *Webster's Third New International Dictionary of the English Language* (1981 edition), which henceforth is abbreviated as *Webster³*. Thus (2) is the typical example:

(2)   ecónomy $_N$] → ecónómic $_A$]

In (2), while the noun *economy* has the primary stress on the antepenult, the corresponding adjective has the primary stress moved onto the penult, the syl-

Chapter 7   Water Finds Its Level   87

lable just before the -*ic* morpheme.

But there are certain exceptions to this general pattern. Observe (3):

(3)   Árabic $_A$]
      Cátholic $_A$]
      lúnatic $_A$]
      pólitic $_A$]

All the words in (3) have the primary stress on the antepenult in spite of the fact that they are all -*ic* adjectives. There are, in fact, other types of exceptions to this pattern. Observe (4) and (5):

(4)   héretic $_{N/A}$], herétic $_A$]
      climácteric $_{N/A}$], climactéric $_{N/A}$]

(5)   rhétoric $_N$]

In (4), we have exceptional [*héretic* $_A$] and [*climácteric* $_A$] as well as pattern-conforming [*herétic* $_A$] and [*climactéric* $_A$]. Note that [*héretic* $_N$] and [*climácteric* $_N$] in (4) and [*rhétoric* $_N$] in (5) are not the -*ic* adjectives but they are -*ic* nouns. We will shortly see their behavior with respect to -*al* suffix below.

English has another suffix -*al*, besides -*ic*, that will convert a noun into an adjective, as in the case of *nature* → *natural*, and these suffixes can be combined to make a new adjectival ending -*ical*, though the meanings of -*ic* adjectives and -*ical* adjectives are slightly different from each other, in some cases. But the important point is that as you can see in (6):

(6)   económic $_A$]
      económical $_A$]
      económically $_{Adv}$]

even in the -*ical* adjectives, and for that matter in the -*ically* adverb, the main stress falls on just the same syllable as that of -*ic* adjectives, i.e. just before the -*ic* morpheme.

Now observe the following cases:

(7)   Cátholic $_A$]   →   cathólically $_{Adv}$]
      lúnatic $_A$]   →   lunátical $_A$], lunátically $_{Adv}$]
      pólitic $_A$]   →   polítical $_A$], polítically $_{Adv}$]

88   A Dynamic Study of Some Derivative Processes in English Grammar

For all their irregularity in primary stress placement, the words *Cátholic, lúnatic* and *pólitic* all conform to the standard regularity when they are in the form of *-ical* adjectives and also in the form of *-ically* adverbs. *Pólitic,* for example, has the irregular placement of primary stress on the antepenult, whereas the derivationally related *polítical* and *polítically* have the regular placement of the primary stress on the syllable just before the *-ic* morpheme.

Now let us turn our attention to the three nouns in (4) and (5). We have the following *-ical* adjectives, which are directly or indirectly related to these three nouns, respectively.

(8)   herétical ₐ]

(9)   climactérical ₐ]

(10)   rhetórical ₐ]

It is unclear whether the adjective *herétical* is directly derived from the noun [*heretic* ₙ] or from the adjective [*heretic* ₐ], but it is definitely clear that the adjective *herétical* has received the primary stress on the syllable right before the morpheme *-ic.* The same observation applies to the adjective *climactérical,* which is derived from either the noun [*climacteric* ₙ] or the adjective [*climacteric* ₐ]. But, the *-ical* adjective *climactérical,* irrespective of the direct source of it, has received the primary stress on the antepenult, the syllable right before the morpheme *-ic.* Lastly, the adjective *rhetórical* falls in the same line of argument except that it is derived from the noun *rhétoric,* since there is no adjective *rhetoric* in English.

The suffixes *-ize* and *-ism* do not affect the placement of the primary stress in the stems to which these morphemes are attached, as exemplified below:

(11)   cháracter → cháracterize
       indústrial → indúsrialize

(12)   Américan → Américanism
       multicúltural → multicúlturalism

But observe the following:

(13)   Árabic → Arábicize, Arábicism

(14) Cátholic → Cathólicism

The words of irregular stress placement, i.e. *Árabic* and *Cátholic*, have now conformed to the regular pattern such that the primary stress falls on the syllable just before the -*ic* morpheme when they have -*ize* morpheme or -*ism* morpheme attached to the end of their stems.

So far we have seen the cases in which exceptions when involved in the further process of derivation take to the courses designed for the normal, standard and regular expressions of the language.

7.2.2. Vowel Quality 'Restoration'

American English has a general tendency to have, as a short stressed vowel, the phonetic form [ɑ] for the letter -*o*-, as shown in (15). Phonetic facts are based on *Webster³*, but the phonetic representations employed here are after IPA notation.

(15) pot   [pɑt]
     top   [tɑp]
     cop   [kɑp]
     botany   [bɑtəni]
     dot   [dɑt]
     God   [gɑd]
     hot   [hɑt]

The words in (15) are an extremely small part of the huge number of English words that illustrate this general tendency of spelling-pronunciation relationship.

There are, however, a certain number of exceptions to this sound-spelling correspondence. Observe (16):

(16) abóve
     cóme
     cómfort
     cómpany
     dóne
     dóve
     frónt

glóve
hóney
Lóndon
lóve
móney
mónkey
móther
óther
són
wónder

The words in (16) all have a short stressed vowel spelled as -o-. The exceptional quality in this case is that the vowel in question is [ʌ], but is never [ɑ]. See Yasui (1955: 96–99) for the origins of this exceptional quality.

Now, if some of the words in (16) go through further derivational processes, we find seriously interesting facts uncovered.

(17) frónt → fróntal, fróntier

móney → mónetarily, mónetary, mónetize

The vowel in *frónt* is stressed and it is [ʌ], but the stressed vowels in *fróntal* and *fróntier* can be either [ʌ] or [ɑ], according to *Webster³*. The same is true with the word *money* and its related words. The stressed vowel in *money* is [ʌ] but never [ɑ]. This exceptional practice, however, is not always carried over into the derivationally related words, i.e. in the words *monetarily, monetary* and *monetize*. *Webster³* cites both [ɑ] and [ʌ] for the stressed vowels in *mónetarily, mónetary* and *mónetize*.

Now some words are in order here. Observe carefully the order of the vowels cited in *Webster³*. As for the stressed vowels in *frontal* and *frontier*, *Webster³* cites, first, [ʌ] and secondly [ɑ] with such editorial comments as *sometimes* and *also* before the vowel [ɑ]. This fact shows that in these words, the stressed vowel is more likely the original one [ʌ] rather than [ɑ]. And this case of the words derived from *front* is in sharp contrast with the case of *money* and its related words. *Webster³* cites, for the stressed vowels in *mónetarily* and *mónetary*, [ɑ] and [ʌ] in the order presented here. And as for the stressed vowel in *mónetize*, *Webster³* cites, first, [ɑ] and secondly [ʌ] with such an editorial comment as *sometimes* before the vowel [ʌ]. These facts imply that the vowel that never showed up in *money*, i.e. [ɑ], appears as the most frequent vowel, but the original vowel [ʌ] appears as the less frequent vowel, in such derivationally related words as *mónetarily*, *mónetary* and *mónetize*. Vowel variations in the words of (17) point to the fact that the vowel quality change is not a unitary phenomenon, but it leaves room for certain variations. Given such variations, we should predict, furthermore, that there will be cases where the vowel quality change has not been triggered even when the word in question has gone through an additional process of derivation. And it is, in fact, the case. See the paragraph after the next one.

Examples in (17) show that exceptional vowel quality may be so modified that it should be in tune with other numerous normal patterns when the words of which the very exceptional vowel is part are further derivationally processed. Regular vowel quality may be restored, 'restoration' being such that the exceptional character is abolished when it is put into a derivationally new process, and then we have the regular character in place.

Notice that what is meant in the preceding paragraph is not such as to say that existence of a new derivational process is a sufficient condition for the regular vowel quality to be restored. To the contrary. I rather maintain that existence of a new derivational process is a necessary condition for the phenomena to be realized. As an illustration, see the words in (18), which are derived from some of the words in (16).

(18) accómpany
      cómfortable
      hóneymoon
      Lóndoner
      lóvely
      mónkeyfy
      wónderer, wónderful, wónderland

All the stressed vowels in (18) are [ʌ], but never [ɑ]. If existence of a certain new derivational process is a sufficient condition for the restoration of the regular quality of the vowel, then our prediction fails. All the words in (18) underwent a certain derivational process, but never gained the regular quality. Thus we should regard the existence of a new derivational process as a necessary condition for the restoration of the regular quality. For this issue, see Nakazawa (1997, 1999a, 2000a, chapter 2 and Part III of this thesis) and the

92   *A Dynamic Study of Some Derivative Processes in English Grammar*

references cited there.

One might attempt a different approach to the vowel quality restoration, the phenomena illustrated in (17). For example, one might be tempted to explain the phenomena in terms of such notions as vowel harmony, assimilation, dissimilation and so on. I will not go into the detail here, but it is definitely clear that if you look at the words in (17) and (18), you cannot draw a convincing phonological demarcation line that separates the vowel quality restoration group from the other non-restoration goroup. So the phonological account fails, which leaves our account promising, i.e. an account such that exceptions may sometimes resort to regularity.

7.3. Exceptions and Regularities in Lexicon/Morphology

English has a number of irregular plural nouns like those in (19):

(19)   antenna   →   antennae
       foot   →   feet
       goose   →   geese
       life   →   lives

But once a word has acquired a new derivative meaning, i.e. the meaning extended from the original basic meaning, regularity surfaces. The original meaning of *antenna* is a sensory appendage of an insect, but today it refers to a metallic device for sending or receiving radio waves. Now, if *antenna* is used to mean the former sense, its plural form is *antennae* or, as a recent innovation, *antennas*, whereas if it is used to mean the latter sense, its plural form is nothing but *antennas* (or, at least, most of the times). If *foot* means the terminal part of a leg, then its plural is *feet*, but when it means sediment or dregs, or a footlight, its plural is *foots*. Cf. *Webster*[3] and *Random House Unabridged Dictionary Second Edition* (1993 edition), which henceforth is abbreviated as *RHD*[2]. If *goose* means a kind of bird, then its plural is *geese*, but once it is used to mean a poke between buttocks or a tailor's smoothing iron with a curved handle (cf. *Webster*[3] and *RHD*[2]), its plural becomes *gooses*. The expression *still life* has as its plural form either *still lives* or *still lifes* (cf. Adams (1973: 10)).

Observing the facts given above, we certainly feel safe to conclude that the nouns with irregular plurals take to the standard, normal and regular procedure and mould the regular plurals when they go through a semantic extension or a metaphorical extortion.

7.4. Exceptions and Regularities in Morphology/Syntax

The last section, i.e. §7.3, has dealt with the inflection of nouns, more specifically the plural forms of nouns. In this section, we consider the inflection of verbs, more specifically the past and the past participial forms of verbs.

English has a certain number of irregular verbs, one of which is the verb *blow*. As the irregular past and the irregular past participial forms for *blow*, we have *blew* and *blown*, respectively. But according to *Webster's New World Dictionary of American English Third College Edition* (1988 edition; henceforth *WNW*) and *Random House Webster's College Dictionary* (1991 edition; henceforth *RHW*), the verb *blow* has the regular past and past participial form *blowed*, when it means "to damn." And *Webster³* cites the senses "ignore, disregard" for the verb *blow* and it gives the example in which the regular *blowed* is used. See the following:

(20)   Well, I'll be blowed!   (*RHW*, s.v. *blow*)

(21)   Risk be blowed.   (*Webster³*, s.v. *blow*)

In (20) and (21), we see the irregular verb *blow* transformed into a regular verb when it went through a semantic extension.

Next, while the verb *fly* has irregular inflections, i.e. *flew* and *flown,* it has the regular form *flied* when it means "to hit a fly ball in baseball" and "to hang or raise (scenery) on the stage". Cf. *RHW* and *Webster³*, s.v. *fly*.

Thirdly, the verb *shine* has the regular form *shined* for the past and the past participial inflection when it means "to make (shoes) bright by polishing", even though it otherwise has the irregular form *shone*. Cf. *WNW, RHW* and *Webster³*, s.v. *shine*.

Once again, the verbs *fly* and *shine* have been transformed to regular verbs when they have gone through a semantic extension.

The same type of phenomena can be observed when an irregular verb constitutes the second part of a compound verb, as in *babysit, ghostwrite, sightsee,* etc. Shimamura (1985) picked out a dozen such verbs, which are listed in (22), and examined their behaviors as to their inflectional regularity.

(22) babysit
broadcast
daydream
freethrow
ghostwrite
joyride
pinch-hit
proofread
sightsee
skydive
skywrite
spoon-feed

Shimamura consulted five native speakers of English; four are American, one Canadian. The result is: Of all the compound verbs in (22), only two retained the same irregularity with their begetters; the two verbs are *proofread* and *spoon-feed.* This means that all five informants approved, as the past and past participial inflections, *proofread* and *spoon-fed,* and rejected **proofreaded* and **spoonfeeded* altogether. And Shimamura shows that the informants' individual differences have prevailed among the rest of the verbs in (22). Some approve only the non-finite forms of the verb, while others approve of both non-finites and the present tense form of the verb but rejects the past tense forms altogether, be it a regular past or an irregular one. And still another group of informants accept both the regular past and the irregular past. And, furthermore, some other informants accept only one of the past forms, either a regular past or an irregular one. So goes the complexity. See Shimamura (1985) for the detail.

But one thing is evidently clear from Shimamura's observation: there are cases where an irregular verb has the regular past and past participial form of the verb when it constitutes the second part, i.e. head, of the entire compound verb. Thus exceptional items—irregular verbs—may sometimes find the normal procedure—regular inflections—when they have undergone a grammatical derivation, i.e. to be a part of a compound verb.

Chapter 7   Water Finds Its Level   95

7.5.   Exceptions and Regularities in Syntax

7.5.1.   Nominal Adverbial

In English, not only adverbs but many other syntactic categories assume the adverbial function. Noun phrase is one such case as illustrated below:

(23)   John arrived in Tokyo *this morning.*

(24)   This Thomas understands racism and bigotry *the way an owl knows the night.*   (*Newsweek* Sept. 16, 1991)

The italicized parts in (23) and (24) are, from a categorial point of view, noun phrases, while their function is adverbial. So if we see them from a categorial viewpoint, they are adverbial noun phrases, whereas if we see them from a functional viewpoint, they are nominal adverbials. As for the classification of nominal adverbials and their related issues, see Nakazawa (2000b) and the references cited there. What is important here in this context is that, from a synactic-categorial point of view, the most basic category that assumes an adverbial function is adverb, so a nominal adverbial is a less basic, if not exceptional, category that assumes the adverbial function.

As adverbs modify verbs, verb phrases and adjectives, among others, so do nominal adverbials modify verbs, verb phrases and adjectives. And when an adverb modifies an adjective, the basic syntactic principle is adjacency and the word order is such that the modifier comes first and then comes the modified, as exemplified in (25):

(25)   Mary is *really pretty.*

But when a nominal adverbial modifies an adjective, there appears a different configuration. Observe (26):

(26)   The alternatives to treating Passive as applicable to [$_{V'}$ Adv V′] are thus to treat *intentionally* in *being intentionally ignored* as moved from some other position or to treat *intentionally* in that combination as being not an ad-V′ but an ad-V. I will resist the former possibility as long as possible, since it would reduce considerably the possibilities for explaining rather than merely describing the distribution of

adverbs. The other alternative appears to have the same implications as our original analysis regarding the distribution of adverbs, and in adopting it one can exploit McConnell-Ginet's rule for the relation between ad-V and ad-V′ senses of adverbs, though one should at least worry about the fact that there is no clear distinction between the ad-V′ sense of *intentionally* and a putative ad-V sense the way that there is a fairly clear distinction between two such senses of *carefully*.　　　　　　　　　　　　　　　　　　　(McCawley (1988: 649))

In the third sentence of the passage in (26), there is a nominal adverbial "*the way that there is a fairly clear distinction between two such senses of* carefully." And our next concern is: What does this nominal adverbial modify? A careful reading will show that the answer is the adjective *clear* in the clause "*there is no clear distinction between the ad-V′ sense of* intentionally *and a putative ad-V sense.*"[3] Now remember the basic word order for the modifier and the modified: the modifier first, the modified second, both being adjacent to each other. Remember also that a nominal adverbial is rather an exceptional adverbial phrase. So the configuration of the modifier and the modified in (26) is strikingly exceptional in that the modifier and the modified are not adjacent to each other, the modified comes first and the modifier comes second, and the modifier is displaced far away from the modified.

　　The next question we should ask is: Why was it made possible for us to

---

[3] Here, by "a careful reading," I mean this. A reader may be tempted to believe that a nominal adverbial "*the way that there is a fairly clear distinction between two such senses of* carefully" modifies "*there is no clear distinction between ad-V′ sense of* intentionally *and a putative ad-V sense.*" According to this 'tempted' view, the whole sentence would mean (i):

(i)　The manner of existence of a clear distinction between ad-V′ sense of *intentionally* and a putative ad-V sense is not the same as the manner of existence of a fairly clear distinction between two such senses of *carefully*.

But, actually, the sentence (i) is rather awkward. The whole sentence should rather mean (ii):

(ii)　The degree of clarity of the distinction between ad-V′ sense of *intentionally* and a putative ad-V sense is not the same as the degree of clarity of the distinction between two such senses of *carefully*: the latter is much greater than the former.

If this interpretation is correct, the relevant logical relation of this sentence is (iii):

(iii)　The distinction between ad-V′ sense of *intentionally* and a putative ad-V sense is NOT [clear [the way that there is a fairly clear distinction between two such senses of *carefully*]].

arrive at this specific type of exceptional configuration? The answer lies, it seems, in the syntactic regularity that dictates that the heavy noun phrase that has appeared in the middle of a sentence may or must be displaced away and find its own place at the end of the clause, a process called Extraposition. Therefore we conclude that the exceptional nominal adverbial in (26) has found a normal, standard position at the end of the clause, just like heavy phrases are normally extraposed clause-finally.

7.5.2. Grammatical Naturalization

Most generally speaking, adjectives modify nouns both syntactically and semantically, as in the phrase in (27):

(27) a red flower

where *red* modifies *flower* both syntactically and semantically. However, there are cases where an adjective modifies the following noun syntactically but not semantically at all. Nakazawa (2001b, 2004, chapter 4 of this thesis) has pointed out such cases, which he called Grammatical Naturalization. Some of the typical examples of this phenomenon are shown in (28)–(30). For the entire picture of, and a possible approach to, this linguistic phenomenon, see Nakazawa (2001b, 2004, chapter 4 of this thesis).

(28) a. They drank a *quick* cup of tea.
     b. They quickly drank a cup of tea.

(Nunberg et al. (1994: 500, n. 14))

(29) a. A neighborhood group locked *legal* horns with the Berkeley school district yesterday. (Deborah Beccue, *The Daily Californian* Dec. 5, 1991 [truncated from a longer sentence])
     b. In the domain of legal matters, a neighborhood group locked horns with the Berkeley school district yesterday.

(30) a. Sam kicked the *proverbial* bucket.   (Chafe (1968: 124))
     b. Sam kicked the bucket and it was in the proverbial manner.

The italicized adjectives in the a-sentences of (28)–(30) do modify the following nouns, but they never function as the semantic modifiers of the following nouns. Semantically speaking, they rather modify the entire sentence or the

98 *A Dynamic Study of Some Derivative Processes in English Grammar*

verb phrase, acting as sentential / VP adverbials, as the paraphrases show; b-sentences being paraphrases of a-sentences. What is striking in these cases is that once the adverbial modifier is transformed into an adjective, this adjective climbs down into the syntactic object of the verb phrase and goes hand in hand with the head noun of the object NP, which means that this adjective mock-behaves as a modifier of the noun following it. This is what we call Grammatical Naturalization, since this adjective, born outside the verb phrase, let alone the object NP of this verb phrase, has now settled in the new foreign land with no kinship around her at all. Remember that "to drink a cup of tea" in (28) is a free phrase, "to lock horns with (someone)" in (29) is an idiom with its entire meaning, some would say, being decomposable; others would say, not being decomposable, and that "to kick the bucket" in (30) is such a hard nut idiom that you cannot break it into syntactic pieces, nor can you into semantic pieces. Grammatical Naturalization, nevertheless, happens in each and every corner of the verb phrases in (28)–(30).

When put in the semantic perspective, Grammatical Naturalization is extremely exceptional, but when put in the syntactic perspective, Grammatical Naturalization is not surprising. Grammatically Naturalized adjectives find their most comfortable place in front of the noun: this is nothing but a syntactic regularity. The example in (27) is the crudest instance of this regularity and the examples in (28)–(30) the sophisticated ones.

7.6. Theoretical Issues

So far in the preceding sections, we have observed that exceptions may sometimes cancel their exceptional features and take to the regular courses when confronted with the additional burden of going further away into a new process of derivation. This section touches upon some theoretical issues that might arise in describing, analyzing and explaining this type of phenomena.

Cognitivists might want to see any motivation for every fractional piece of linguistic phenomena. But consider the vowel [ʌ] in *money.* The vowel is just asking for trouble if, instead of remaining as it is, it circumvents the easiest goal and takes the longer way to the other goal.

(31)   money [mʌni]

Chapter 7　Water Finds Its Level　99

(32)　monetize [mʌnətaiz]

(33)　monetize [mɑnətaiz]

What I mean is that it should be much easier for (31) to arrive at (32) than it is for (31) to arrive at (33). Thus (31) is least motivated to arrive at (33), but this is what actually happens. Or consider the Grammatically Naturalized adjectives, which are discussed in the last section. They have the least motivation to arrive at the place where they have no semantic relationship around there. But this is what actually happens.

The same line of arguments might apply to the rigorous formal linguists' ideas, e.g. economy. In order to argue for or against a particular theory, you need a specific, full-fledged version of it to apply it to concrete empirical cases. But as far as our general instinct goes, the cases so far examined, or the cases of (31)–(33) and Grammatically Naturalized adjectives, to name a few, all seem to be against the principle of economy. If this intuition is correct, then we need some other way to look for a better answer.

Or if the current rigorous formal linguists' theories are output-oriented theories, as Kajita terms them in Kajita (1997, 2001) and elsewhere, we wonder why (31) has an exceptional vowel [ʌ]. For, if (31) had the regular vowel [ɑ], it could directly arrive at the output state of (33). But the reality is that (31) has the irregular vowel [ʌ]. Or if output-oriented theorists say that having the vowel [ɑ] is the output condition for the letter -o- with a primary stress on it, then what should we do with the examples in (16) and (18)?

Furthermore, if output theorists are correct, we wonder why Grammatically Naturalized adjectives step into the slots where semantic consistency is outlawed. The output state should have guaranteed the semantic consistency, but, as we can see, the result is catastrophically inconsistent from a semantic point of view.

So the process-oriented theories, as Kajita's terminology goes, seem promising. Process-oriented theories dictate the possible transitions from one state to the next. The exceptional vowel [ʌ] in (31) will find, in the next stage, the regular vowel [ɑ] as the possible vowel for the letter -o- with a primary stress on it. And as for the cases of Grammatical Naturalization, it seems likely that once the sentential / VP adverbial has been turned into an adjective, this adjective will find the prenominal position as the best possible site for her in the next step of derivation, because [Det A N] is the most standard and prevalent nominal sturucture in English.

Other linguistic phenomena taken up in this chapter may, in my view, fall within the range of the process-oriented theories. The purpose of this chapter has been to show the divergent categories of linguistic phenomena and to suggest that the generalizations induced from each type of linguistic facts and analyses do not belong to the components these facts and and analyses are in, but rather they should be explained from a more abstract point of view. And one such viewpoint seems the process-oriented theories.

Chapter 8

The *Dungeon* Construction: A Syntactic Hapax Legomenon

8.1. Regularity and Irregularity in Exceptions

It is often said that there is no rule without exceptions, and indeed I believe this is true. Language has a whole variety of exceptions but in my view, there are at least two types of exceptions: one is the type where we find no systematicity or regularity in the exceptions concerned, and the other is the type where we can surely manage to analyze those exceptions. As examples for the former type, we may cite those in (1). And as for the latter type, we may refer to the 'exception to the irregular plurals,' as exemplified in (2).

(1) a. *went* (past tense form of *go*)
    b. kick the bucket (= 'die')
    c. kingdom come (= 'the next world,' 'heaven')

(2) a. mouse (rodent): mice vs. mouse (PC device): mouses
    b. antenna (insect's organ): antennae vs. antenna (aerial): antennas

Exceptions in (1) are the kind of examples we call idiosyncrasies: we have no other way than to remember them. If we are asked why *go* has the past tense form *went* instead of **goed*, we say "Just remember"; if we are asked why *kick the bucket* means 'die,' we say "Just remember"; and if we are

101

asked why *kingdom come* means 'the next world' or 'heaven,' we say "Just remember."

As for the exceptions in (2), it is true that we have to remember all the 'irregularities' in such a way that although *mouse*, for example, has a 'standard' irregular plural *mice*, we have to remember a distinctly different form *mouses*, quite 'irregularly.' But seen from a different perspective, examples in (2) will lead us to the general principle such that even irregular items are apt to take on a regular garment when they are put into a certain derivational process and become entirely new individual words. This is indeed the case with the examples in (2).[1]

Now, there is another type of irregularity that deserves a systematic analysis. This chapter is an attempt to find a rational way to analyze one of the most recalcitrant syntactic constructions in English grammar, so recalcitrant that we often let the construction go unnoticed though it has much of irregularity. The construction is what we call the *Dungeon* construction.

8.2. The *Dungeon* Construction

The construction we are concerned with in this chapter is illustrated by the examples in (3), and I will henceforth call this construction the *Dungeon* construction.

(3) a. Into the dungeon with the traitors!   (Jackendoff (1973: 347))
    b. Down with the traitors!
    c. Away with you!
    d. Off with {you / your hat / his head}!

The first and foremost peculiar feature of this construction is the interpretation of the phrase [PP *with* NP]. The normal practice of the interpretation of the phrases / sentences involving *with* is such that when followed by an NP, the preposition *with* is used to mean, among others, accompaniment, possession and instrumental. But observe the semantic interpretation of the examples of (3) in the form of rough paraphrases, as shown in (4), respectively:

---

[1] Chapter 7 of this thesis concerns this type of exceptions and points to a general principle that we believe governs these irregular processes.

Chapter 8   The *Dungeon* Construction: A Syntactic Hapax Legomenon   103

(4) a.   "Traitors shall go down into the dungeon!"

    b.   "Traitors shall be down!"

    c.   "You should be away from me!"

    d.   "{You / Your hat / His head} should be off of {me / you / his body}!"

This interpretation is in stark contrast with the normal type of interpretation of *with*, a few of which are exemplified in (5):

(5) a.   We stepped into the dungeon with the tourists.

    b.   Mary walked down the street with her friends.

    c.   John will be away from Tokyo in Hawaii with his wife.

    d.   The thief ran off with the money.

    e.   John sliced cheese with a knife.

In (5a–c), [$_{PP}$ *with* NP] means accompaniment of the object NP in this PP to the subject NP of the entire sentence: in the event where subject in each of these sentences is involved as an agent or theme, NP in [$_{PP}$ *with* NP] accompanies sentential subject.   Thus, *the tourists* accompanies *we* in (5a), *her friends Mary* in (5b), and *his wife John* in (5c).   In (5d), [$_{PP}$ *with* NP] means possession: *the thief* possesses *the money*.   In (5e), [$_{PP}$ *with* NP] means that *a knife* is instrumental: *John* used *a knife* as an instrument.

But in (3), the semantic role of the NP in [$_{PP}$ *with* NP] is unambiguously agent / actor or theme in the event these sentences depict.   Despite the superficial similarity of the sequences of words observed in both (3a–d) and (5a–d), which is shown in (6) below, the behavior of the NP in [$_{PP}$ *with* NP] in the *Dungeon* construction (i.e. (3)) is systematically different from that of the normal construction (i.e. (5)).

(6) a.   ...into the dungeon with NP.

    b.   ...down...with NP.

    c.   ...away...with NP.

    d.   ...off with NP.

So, as Jackendoff admits, this construction is "an especially curious construction in English." (Jackendoff (1973: 347))[2]

---

[2] Jackendoff (1973) does not try to analyze the *Dungeon* construction itself. He only assumes that "no matter how this construction is derived" (Jackendoff (1973: 347)), phrases that stand before *with* are syntactic PPs despite their superficial appearances. As will be

104   *A Dynamic Study of Some Derivative Processes in English Grammar*

Now let us observe the *Dungeon* construction more closely and see how peculiar the construction is. Listed below is a set of peculiar features of the *Dungeon* construction:

(7) a. It is a nonfinite clause.

   b. It has a directional phrase followed by [PP *with* NP].

   c. NP in the PP [PP *with* NP] is a definite NP.

   d. NP in the PP [PP *with* NP] is the agent / actor or theme of the event, or put into syntactic terms, the subject NP in the paraphrase for the construction: *the traitors*, for example, in "Into the dungeon with the traitors!" is the agent / actor or theme, or the subject NP in the paraphrase "The traitors shall go down into the dungeon!"

   e. Though the preposition *with* is used to express a whole variety of meanings and relations such as 'contact,' 'accompaniment,' 'possession,' 'instrumental,' 'circumstantial condition,' and many others, it is never followed by an agent / actor or theme, or a subject NP. But, note well, so it is only when in the *Dungeon* construction.

8.3. Assumptions

Before going into the analysis of the *Dungeon* construction, we need some groundwork for the understanding of the framework we are assuming.

First of all, here in this chapter, or for that matter throughout the thesis, we assume the theoretical framework called Grammatical Dynamism advocated by Kajita (1977, and elsewhere), with certain modifications on it. Second, we assume that there are at least two types of rules, major and minor, the distinction depending on their productivity. Third, we assume that there is some form of extensional dependency among rules, or to use more familiar terms, among 'constructions.'

---

shown in later sections, Jackendoff is in part correct, but in part incorrect.

8.3.1. Grammatical Dynamism

Grammatical Dynamism is a theory that aims to explain language acquisition in such a way as follows: as children acquire language in the step-by-step mode, so the grammar is constructed in the same manner in the mind (or brain) of children; these children grow up to be adults having the final state of a particular grammar, e.g. English grammar. In contrast, Chomsky (1965, 1995, 2013, and elsewhere) assumes a model of theory that claims that language acquisition can be made possible instantaneously, without reference to the intermediate stages between the initial and the final state. Thus Kajita (1997) calls Grammatical Dynamism a process-oriented theory and Chomsky's model an output-oriented theory. And the former is also called a dynamic model (or theory) of grammar or Grammatical Dynamism, while the latter is called an instantaneous model. See Kajita (1977, 1983, 1997, 2002) for the detail.[3]

The theory format of Grammatical Dynamism is shown below:

(8) If the grammar of a language L at stage i, G(L, i), has property P,
     then the grammar of the language at the next stage, G(L, i+1), may
     have property P′.   (Kajita (2002: 161))

(8) can be rephrased in an abstract form as in (9), where A stands for the proposition "the grammar of a language L at stage i, G(L, i), has property P," and B for the proposition "the grammar of the language at the next stage, G(L, i+1), has property P′":

(9) If A, then B is possible.

But, as I discussed in the previous chapters (especially chapters 2 and 3), the format of (8), i.e. that of (9), needs to be modified. Needless to say, the

---

[3] I do not make a comparison here between the process-oriented and the output-oriented theories. See Kajita's works for this topic, and the references cited in Kajita (1992b) for the empirical studies within this framework. See also Kono (2013), which contains in part a discussion on this topic and references other than those in Kajita (1992b). I assume that the process-oriented theory is superior to the output-oriented one in many respects, but especially when we are engaged in the detailed description of a vast variety of linguistic facts and faced with the explanation of how and why these facts are as they are, I strongly believe that the former with certain modifications on it is better.

106   *A Dynamic Study of Some Derivative Processes in English Grammar*

wording of what stands for B and A has to be changed slightly. Thus we assume the format of (10):

(10)   If B, then A;
        where B stands for the proposition "the grammar of a language L at
        stage i (i≠0), G(L, i), has property P'," and A for the proposition "the
        grammar of the language at the stage i-1, G(L, i-1), has property P."

Quite informally stated, (10) should be read as (11):

(11)   If we have a property P' in the grammar G' at a certain stage, then
        we have as a forerunner a property P in the grammar G before that
        stage.

As is clear from the format in (10), A is a necessary condition for B. Note that it is still the case that in (9) A is a necessary condition for B. It seems that the format of (9) may sometimes look misleading, for you may often mistakenly tend to think of A as the sufficient condition for B in the very formulation of (9). But, of course, A is a necessary condition for B even in the formulation of (9). (The latter interpretation is what I call a 'loose' inpterpretation of (9). See §11.1 in chapter 11.)

8.3.2.   Major Rules vs. Minor Rules

We assume that there are at least two types of rules regarding their productivity. They are major rules and minor rules.[4] The criteria for the notions 'major' vs. 'minor' are shown below:

(12)   Criteria for major vs. minor rules
        a. the number of items that undergo the process the rule dictates
        b. the number of derivative or related rules that the "mother" rule accommodates

If the number designated by (12a) is large, the rule is a major rule. If it is

---

[4] The idea of major vs. minor rules that I propose here is my own innovation, but as far as the typology of transformations are concerned, I got no small inspiration from Kajita's (1974: 428–429) "Bunkyoku no kasetsu (Polarization hypothesis [translation from Japanese mine–K.N.])." See also Kajita (1974: 420–428), Lakoff (1970: 30).

Chapter 8   The *Dungeon* Construction: A Syntactic Hapax Legomenon   107

small, it is a minor rule. Similarly, if the number designated by (12b) is large, the rule is a major rule. If it is small, it is a minor rule. Let us illustrate what the criteria mean in the analysis of syntax.

Take, for example, Passive transformation (hereafter abbreviated as Passive when confusion does not arise). The verb *hit*, for example, undergoes the process that Passive dictates. In other words, the verb *hit* governs the passive transformation in the sense that Lakoff (1970: 28) assumed. And there are great many verbs that behave in the same fashion: verbs like *kick, kiss, eat, admire, see, believe, tell* and many others will make a long list of verbs that are used in the passive construction. Therefore, Passive is a major rule. This is due to the criterion (12a).

Next, the active sentence (13a) undergoes Passive, and becomes a passive sentence (13b). See below. Note here, in this chapter, that I assume rules called transformations, and will say, simply for ease of exposition, that a transformation applies to a sentence / construction and the latter is transformed into another sentence / construction, putting aside such technical terms as "phrase structure rules," "structural description / change," "deep / surface structure," or, more recently, "Merge," "Move α," "phase" and many others. Broadly speaking, here I assume that a transformation guarantees the existence of a new construction.

Now, the passive construction (13b) can be 'molded' into other constructions, as shown in (13c, d, e):

(13) a.   John kissed Mary.
      b.   Mary was kissed by John.
      c.   Mary got kissed by John.
      c′. Mary got sick.
      d.   We found Mary kissed by John.
      d′. We found Mary sick.
      e.   We bought cameras made in Japan.
      e′. We bought cameras full of all sorts of accessories.

Part of the passive construction, i.e. *kissed by John*, can be used as a predicate of *get*-passive as in (13c). What this construction means is that once a certain construction is transformed into another construction, this derived construction gives way to another transformation to apply to this derived structure itself. Thus we derive a passive construction, and this passive construction makes it possible for another transformation to apply to (part of) this passive construction: due to Passive, we have the phrase *kissed by John*, and this phrase is put into the slot that an AP fills in the construction (13c') [[$_{NP}$ Mary] [$_V$ got] [$_{AP}$ sick]]. Here, substitution of [*kissed by John*] for [sick] will make (13c). In other words, only by way of applying Passive, can we arrive at the construction (13c). In this sense, we can refer to Passive as a mother rule with respect to the construction (13c). Similarly, Passive is a mother rule to the construction (13d), which is based on the construction (13d') [[$_{NP}$ We] [$_V$ found] [$_{NP}$ Mary] [$_{AP}$ sick]]. Likewise, Passive is a mother rule to (13e), which is based on the construction (13e') [[$_{NP}$ We] [$_V$ bought] [$_{NP}$ cameras] [$_{AP}$ full of all sorts of accessories]]. If we employ Kiparsky's (1968) terminology, we may say that Passive feeds many rules that are responsible for the constructions (13c–e). All this considered, Passive is a major rule. This is due to the criterion (12b).[5]

Our next concern is minor rule. What is it that makes a rule a minor rule? Take, for example, the paradigm of nominal case inflection system in Present-Day English. There are languages that have case systems full of nominal case markers: nominative, genitive, accusative, dative, oblique, instrumental, and much more. But, as far as Present-Day English is concerned, nominal case system is rather poor. Only in pronouns can we find nominative and accusative / dative case, i.e. *I*, *me*; *you*, *you*; *he*, *him*; and others. And only genitive case can we mark it on both pronouns and full NPs, i.e. *my*, *your*, ..., *John's*, *the boy's* and so on. In this case, we can surely confirm that English nominal case system is a minor rule. This is due to the criterion (12a).

In Old and Middle English, there used to be verbs that make impersonal

---

[5] The discussion here might remind you of the thesis "sequential application of transformations." Some of the classical examples that argue for the thesis are as follows:
(i) a.   John fixed up a hamburger for Mary.
    b.   John fixed a hamburger up for Mary.
    c.   John fixed up Mary a hamburger.
    d.   John fixed Mary up a hamburger.
In (i), only through the ordering of "*for*-Dative Shift → Particle Movement," can we arrive at (id). Without this ordering of transformations, how can we avoid interpreting *Mary* in (id) "John fixed Mary up ..." as Patient (or Theme) of the activity verb *fix up*, as in the case of *a hamburger* in (ib) "John fixed a hamburger up ..."? In this chapter, and of course throughout the thesis, we assume that transformations are ordered sequentially.

Chapter 8 The *Dungeon* Construction: A Syntactic Hapax Legomenon 109

construction: verbs like *please* and *like* required dative noun as in (14),[6] where *you* has a dative case:

(14) a. If it please(s) you, ...
     b. If it like(s) you, ...

The number of items that undergo the process of impersonal construction is so small, i.e. *please*, *like*, *seem*, *think* and only a few others, that the rule that derives impersonal construction is a minor rule. This is due to the criterion (12a).

Next, what is it that makes a rule a minor rule due to (12b)? While dative NP of a ditransitive verb undergoes Passive as in (15a), dative NPs of impersonal construction in (14a, b) never do so, as shown in (15b, c):

(15) a. John was given a book. / John was given a chance to go to college.
     b. *If you are pleased, ...
     c. *If you are liked, ...

The rule responsible for the impersonal dative construction feeds no rule, or put differently, it is never a mother rule to any descendant rule. So it is a minor rule. This is due to the criterion (12b)[7].

8.3.3. Extensional Dependency

We have assumed in the previous section that there are feeding relations among rules in the description of English syntactic analysis. The notion of extensional dependency is closely related to this type of relations among constructions. I employ the term 'extension' to technically mean the process shown below, which we discussed in §8.3.1.

---

[6] Examples that follow that are intended to be Old/Middle English are Present-Day English glosses.

[7] Forms like *methinks* and *meseems* are reminiscences of dative *me*, but they are frozen forms, or fossils, so to speak. So the rule responsible for impersonal construction with dative NP is definitely a minor rule in Present-Day English.

To avoid confusion, let me add that though examples like (i) are surely a construction that has a close kinship with "impersonal construction with dative NP," this is not the structure that I call "impersonal construction with dative NP." Contrary to the structure (14a, b), the dative case of *me* in (i) is due to the PP structure in which the very NP is located.

(i) It seems [PP to me] that John will win the race.

(16) If B, then A;

where B stands for the proposition "the grammar of a language L at stage i (i≠0), G(L, i), has property P'," and A for the proposition "the grammar of the language at the stage i-1, G(L, i-1), has property P." (= (10))

Informally stated, a construction C1 can be extended to another construction C2 if C1, as a forerunner, has a certain set of features that C2 could share. In this case, I say that C1 and C2 have extensional dependency, or there is an extensional dependency between C1 and C2.

Notice that extensional dependency is not restricted to that of transformational extension alone. In chapters 2 and 3 we have observed that of phonological extension, in chapters 4 and 6 that of syntactic extension, in chapter 5 that of both phonological and poetic extension, and in chapter 7 that of phonological, lexical and syntactic extension. So, to repeat a line in the previous paragraph, a construction C1 can be extended to another construction C2, whatever the construction may be, i.e. phonological, lexical, syntactic or whatsoever.

8.4. Analysis of the *Dungeon* Construction

8.4.1. *With*-Construction

Observe the sentences in (17). These sentences, each with a PP headed by *with*, constitute a family of *with*-construction.

(17) a. John walked along the street [with Mary].
     b. John pushed the cart [with Mary].
     c. John broke the vase [with a hammer].
     d. John kept on singing [with a hammer in his hand].
     e. I feel so lonely [with you away].
     f. Denice jabs it [with considerable force into our forehead].   (*BNC*)
     g. You didn't have to cook after your day's work, which has to be heavier [with [Frank away] and [you holding the fort]].   (*WBO*)

We propose that the fundamental meaning of *with*-construction is (18). In

Chapter 8   The *Dungeon* Construction: A Syntactic Hapax Legomenon   111

what follows, representations in parentheses, e.g. (&(_, x)) in (18), are intended to mean logical representations.

(18)   The fundamental meaning of *with*-construction [*with* X]: ACCOM-
       PANIMENT
       [BEING-WITH X] or [BEING-SIIDE-BY-SIDE-WITH X]: (&(_, x))

The basic interpretation of (18) is accompaniment, with X being a concrete
object. Thus as an accompaniment interpretation, (17a, b) have paraphrases
like (19a) and (19b), respectively. Notice that (19a) means that John's walking and Mary's walking are in reality independent activities, but it eventually
means that they get together and their activities are regarded as one. Hence
the last logical representation in (19a). In (19b), however, we understand that
the agent of the pushing the cart activity is a single entity, which is the result
of Mary's accompaniment to John, that is to say, the agent is [John AND
Mary].

(19) a.   John walked along the street, and Mary ACCOMPANIED John.
           (WALK (j, ACCOMPANY (m, j))) => (WALK (j, (WALK (m))
           ACCOM)) => (WALK (j&m))[8]
      b.   [John AND Mary] pushed the cart. (PUSH (j&m, c))[8]

Next, we turn to (17c), which is repeated below. When John is side by
side with a hammer, it ultimately means "John HAS a hammer." So the
HAVING interpretation of [*with*-X], i.e. that of possession interpretation, is an
extension from (18) and this interpretation is shown in (20). Furthermore, the
hammer John has is used as an instrument. So the possession interpretation
(20) is further extended to (21), an instrumental interpretation. So, as a possession interpretation, and at the same time as an instrumental interpretation,
(17c) has a paraphrase like (19c) below.

(17) c.   John broke the vase [with a hammer].

(20)   The extended meaning of *with*-construction [*with* X]: POSSESSION
       [HAVING X]: (HAVE (_, x))

(21)   The extended meaning of *with*-construction [*with* X]: INSTRU-

---

[8] For purposes of exposition, here I write (j&m), instead of (&(j, m)).

MENTAL

[HAVING $X_{\text{INSTRUMENTAL}}$]: (HAVE (__ , x_{INST}))

(19) c. John HAD a hammer and broke the vase using the hammer as an INSTRUMENT. (BREAK (j, v, (HAVE (j, h_{INST}))))

Next, we focus on the interpretation of (17d), which is repeated below. The paraphrase of (17d) is (19d), and we can clearly see this is a kind of extension from those of (19a, b, c) in the sense that John HAS a hammer (cf. (19c)) and at the same time John's having a hammer ACCOMPANIES John's activity (cf. (19a, b)). Thus (17d) has a paraphrase like (19d), as both a possession and an accompaniment interpretation. An accompanying condition like the case in (17d) and (19d), we call it a 'circumstantial condition' in the following pages of this chapter.

(17) d. John kept on singing [with a hammer in his hand].

(19) d. John kept on singing, and John's HAVING a hammer in his hand ACCOMPANIED his activity. (SING (j, (HAVE (j, ham, han_{LOC})) CIRCUM COND))

Now, it should be clear that (17d) is an extension from (17a, b, c). And it is important to note that X in the *with*-construction [*with* X] in (17d) is no longer a concrete object, as it was in (17a, b, c), but it is an abstract accompanying condition (*a hammer in his hand*) here in (17d). This is a semantic extension from (20). See (22).

(22) The extended meaning of *with*-construction [*with* X]: CIRCUM-STANTIAL CONDITION

[HAVING X CIRCUMSTANTIAL CONDITION]: (HAVE (__ , x))CIRCUM COND

From a syntactic point of view, (17d) embodies another type of extension: the internal structure of X is extended from a mono-structure to a multi-structure. In (17a, b, c), X in [*with* X] was a single constituent, but now in (17d), X is a 'clausal' structure. Recall the logical representation of (20), where we find a significant development in the process of extension. That is to say: while the syntactic structure of (20) is [*with* [$_{\text{NP}}$ *a hammer*]], the logical counterpart of it is "(HAVE (__ , x))," which means that the latter is a two-place predicate. This fact means that though the structure [*with* [$_{\text{NP}}$ *a hammer*]] looks as if it requires a single syntactic argument NP, the logical representation is such that it is clausal, i.e. it requires two arguments. This is one of the motivations that trigger extension. Thus, the instrumental interpretation of [*with* [$_{NP}$ *a hammer*]] with its logically clausal meaning leads to the extended circumstantial conditional construction [*with* [$_{NP}$ *a hammer*] [$_{PP}$ *in his hand*]], where the structure is clausal both syntactically and logically. So I agree with Sakakibara (1982) and McCawley (1983) in that we assume that the constituent structure of the *with*-construction when it has a circumstantial conditional interpretation, is clausal. That is it has the structure like this: *with* followed by a nonfinite (sometimes verbless) clausal structure, which, in syntactic terms, means [*with* [NP XP]].[9] Thus the phrase [*with a hammer in his hand*] in (17d) can be paraphrased as (HAVE (j, ham, han$_{LOC}$)), where an argument of locative adjunct "han$_{LOC}$" is added. The latter structure in fact has an extended interpretation such as [HAMMER BE IN-HIS-HAND] and its logical representation is (BE (ham, han$_{LOC}$))CIRCUM COND. See (19d′) below.

(23)   The extended meaning of *with*-construction [*with* [$_X$ NP PP]]: CLAUSAL

[NP BE PP]: (BE (np, pp$_{LOC}$)) CIRCUM COND

(19) d′.   (SING (j, (BE (ham, han$_{LOC}$)) CIRCUM COND))

Now, we go to the interpretation of (17e), which is repeated below. The meaning of the *with*-construction here is that of (22), i.e. (23), above, and it is further extended to mean reason of an action or cause of the event that happened. The latter meaning is given in (24) and the paraphrase for (17e) is (19e) below.

(17) e.   I feel so lonely [with you away].

(24)   The extended meaning of *with*-construction [*with* NP XP]: REASON / CAUSE

---

[9] Nonfiniteness of the clause in *with*-construction is presumably in part motivated by the existence of a variety of nonfinite 'small clauses' in English.

   (i) a.   John found [Mary sick].
      b.   John found [Mary on the bed].
      c.   John found [Mary sick in bed].
      d.   John found [Mary sleeping on the bed].
      e.   John found [Mary thrown onto the bed].

[NP XP]$_{\text{REASON/CAUSE}}$: ((BE (np, xp$_{\text{LOC}}$)) CIRCUM COND) REASON/CAUSE

(19) e. I feel so lonely BECAUSE you are away. (FEEL (i, (LONELY (i)), (((BE (y, away$_{\text{LOC}}$)) CIRCUM COND) REASON/CAUSE)))

Next, how about the interpretation of (17f), which is repeated below? The meaning of the *with*-construction here is essentially that of (22) above, that is, it means a circumstantial condition as it does in (17e). But, if we take into account the internal structure semantics of the phrase [*with* [NP XP]], the paraphrase of [*with* [NP XP]] in (17f) is significantly different from that in (17e). See the paraphrase of (17f), i.e. (19f) below.

(17) f. Denice jabs it [with considerable force into our forehead].

(19) f. Denice jabs it and Denice DIRECTED considerable force INTO our forehead. (JAB (d, i, (GO (force, PATH [SOURCE(__), GOAL(forehead)]))) CIRCUM COND))

Let us highlight the difference between (19e) and (19f), focusing on the logical representations for the structure [*with* [NP XP]]:

(25) The difference between (19e) and (19f) with respect to [*with* [NP XP]]

    a. (19e): "with you away" ((BE (y, away$_{\text{LOC}}$)) CIRCUM COND)

    b. (19f): "with considerable force into our forehead" ((GO (force, PATH [SOURCE(__), GOAL(forehead)])) CIRCUM COND)

We could furthermore abstract away incidentals from (25a, b) and obtain the clearer picture of the difference:

(26) The abstracted difference between (19e) and (19f) with respect to [*with* [NP XP]]

    a. (19e): "with x y" (BE (x, y_{LOC})) CIRCUM COND

    b. (19f): "with x y" (GO (x, $y_{\text{DIRECTION}}$)) CIRCUM COND

Now we can see that there is a *with*-construction of a circumstantial condition interpretation that has a clausal internal structure and that this type of *with*-construction has two semantic types: one is (26a) and the other (26b).[10]

---

[10] It may be possible that we have an alternative interpretation of (17f) such as the one in

Chapter 8   The *Dungeon* Construction: A Syntactic Hapax Legomenon   115

Let us finally look at (17g), which is repeated below. (17g) has two *with*-constructions conjoined at the end of the sentence, and they each have a circumstantial interpretation. The first of these has the same interpretation as that of (26a), but the second has the interpretation that can hardly be either (26a) or (26b). Rather, it is the interpretation that we find in the paraphrase of (17g), i.e. (19g).

(17) g.   You didn't have to cook after your day's work, which has to be heavier [with [Frank away] and [you holding the fort]].

(19) g.   You didn't have to cook after your day's work, and cooking has to be heavier BECAUSE Frank is away and you are holding the fort. (($(~\square$(COOK (y))) ((($BE (f, away$_{LOC}$)) CIRCUM COND) & ((HOLD (y, f)) CIRCUM COND) REASON/CAUSE))

The logical representation that corresponds to [*with you holding the fort*] in (17g) is found at the end of (19g), i.e. (HOLD (y, f)) CIRCUM COND, which is repeated in (27a). With incidentals taken away, (HOLD (y, f)) CIRCUM COND becomes an abstract form like (27b) below:

(27) a.   (19g) "with you holding the fort": (HOLD (y, f)) CIRCUM COND
     b.   Abstract form of (19g) "with x [$_{VP}$ v y]": (V (x, y)) CIRCUM COND

Notice that one feature that specifically characterizes the *with*-construction in (27b), i.e. "with x [$_{VP}$ v y]," is the fact that VP is always nonfinite, according to which v should always be nonfinite, too.

Now, let us briefly review the process of constructional extension observed in the *with*-construction in (17). See below, where (17a–g) correspond to (19a–g), respectively:

(i):
    (i)   Denice [jabs it [with considerable force] [into our forehead]].
Under this interpretation, (17f) no longer has the structure (26b). But there are cases where their interpretations do have the structure (26b). See, for example, (30l, m) in §8.4.2 and (ii) below:
    (ii)   [With the bike into the corner and turned], the rider is thinking of one thing only
           from now on — getting on to the throttle as soon as possible.   (*BNC*)
Note that a paraphrase of the bracketed part of (ii) looks like (iii):
    (iii)   The bike GOES into the corner and the bike GETS/IS turned.
The underlined portion of (iii) has the structure (26b).

(19) a. (WALK (j, ACCOMPANY (m, j))) => (WALK (j, (WALK (m)) ACCOM)) => (WALK (j&m))

b. (PUSH (j&m, c))

c. (BREAK (j, v, (HAVE (j, h$_{INST}$))))

d′. (SING (j, (BE (hammer, hand$_{LOC}$)) CIRCUM COND))

e. (FEEL (i, (LONELY (i)), (((BE (y, away$_{LOC}$)) CIRCUM COND) REASON/CAUSE)))

f. (JAB (d, i, (GO (force, PATH [SOURCE(__), GOAL(forehead)])) CIRCUM COND))

g. ((~□(COOK (y))) (((BE (f, away$_{LOC}$)) CIRCUM COND) & ((HOLD (y, f)) CIRCUM COND) REASON/CAUSE))

If we focus only on the *with*-construction itself and pick out the relevant portions from (19), then the result is (28):

(28) Logical representations for the *with*-constructions in (17)

a. (j&m)

b. (j&m)

c. (HAVE (j, h$_{INST}$))

d. ((BE (hammer, hand$_{LOC}$)) CIRCUM COND)

e. ((BE (y, away$_{LOC}$)) CIRCUM COND)

f. ((GO (force, PATH [SOURCE(__), GOAL(forehead)])) CIRCUM COND)

g. ((HOLD (y, f)) CIRCUM COND)

Furthermore, if we put the tentative formulation "(j&m)" back into the authentic one "&(j, m)" and abstract away incidentals from the representations above, we obtain the abstract forms for the very *with*-constructions. See (29):

(29) Abstract logical representations for the *with*-constructions in (17)

a. & (x, y)

b. & (x, y)

c. HAVE (x, y)

d. (BE (x, y$_{LOC}$)) CIRCUM COND

e. (BE (x, y$_{LOC}$)) CIRCUM COND

f. (GO (x, y$_{DIRECTION}$)) CIRCUM COND

g. (V (x, y)) CIRCUM COND

Chapter 8   The *Dungeon* Construction: A Syntactic Hapax Legomenon   117

Now, recall the extension format (16) in §8.3.3, which is repeated below:

(16)   If B, then A;

where B stands for the proposition "the grammar of a language L at stage i (i≠0), G(L, i), has property P'," and A for the proposition "the grammar of the language at the stage i-1, G(L, i-1), has property P." (= (10))

As I stated there, an informal formulation of (16) is as follows: a construction C1 can be extended to another construction C2 if C1, as a forerunner, has a certain set of features that C2 could share.

Let us see how the constructions in (29) are extended.   First, (29a) (= (29b)) has the feature "PREDICATE (x, y)," and this is the very feature (29c) shares with (29a, b).   Next, "HAVE (x, y)" in (29c) implies the side-by-side relation of x and y, i.e. an 'accompaniment' relation, and this is the very feature (29d) (= (29 e)) shares with (29c).   Thirdly, "(BE (x, y_{LOC}))" in (29d) (= (29 e)) has the feature "PREDICATE (x, y_{SPACE})," and this is the very feature (29f) shares with (29d) (= (29 e)).   Finally, "HAVE (x, y)" in (29c) has the feature "V (x, y)," and this is the very feature (29g) shares with (29c), or to be precise, it is the identical feature that (29g) has.   Needless to say, all *with*-constructions in (17) share such basic features as: (i) the construction is headed by the specific lexical item *with*; (ii) the construction is of the structure [PP *with* X]; and (iii) the structure [PP *with* X] as a whole does not come into play directly in the argument structure of the main verb of the sentence to which the construction is attached.[11]

We have so far demonstrated that there exist extensional dependencies in

---

[11] Just in case, let me add a few words regarding the third feature, "(iii) the structure [PP *with* X] as a whole does not come into play directly in the argument structure of the main verb of the sentence to which the construction is attached." Take, for example, the sentence (17b) "John pushed the cart [with Mary]." The argument structure of this sentence is roughly [NP V NP], and it is no different from that of the sentence "John pushed the cart." The only difference is that the subject NP consists of one noun in one case but two in the other. No more, or no less. Therefore, the argument structure of the main verb is intact with or without this type of *with*-construction.

Examples like (i) below are not the sentences with the *with*-construction under investigation.

(i)   a.   John has a close kinship [with Mary]. (K (j, m))
      b.   John is familiar [with Japanese animé]. (F (j, a))

118   *A Dynamic Study of Some Derivative Processes in English Grammar*

the family of *with*-construction shown in (17). And if we use the notions employed in §8.3.2, i.e. major vs. minor rules, we can say that rules responsible for the family of *with*-construction are major rules.

Here is a table given below for a quick review to see how the *with*-construction in (17) is extended from the basic accompaniment interpretation to the derivative circumstantial conditional interpretation. From a semantic point of view, the structure as a whole is extended from 'accompaniment of objects' to 'accompaniment of events'. From a syntactic point of view, the structure after *with* is extended from a single NP structure to a nonfinite clausal structure, i.e. [NP XP].

Table 1: How the *with*-construction is extended in the examples of (17)

	Phrase	Syntactic structure	Logical representation
(17a)	"with Mary"	[*with* NP]	$\& \ (x, y)$
(17b)	"with Mary"	[*with* NP]	$\& \ (x, y)$
(17c)	"with a hammer"	[*with* NP]	HAVE (x, y)
(17d)	"with a hammer in his hand"	[*with* NP PP]	HAVE (x, y, z_{LOC}) => (BE $(x, y_{LOC}))$ CIRCUM COND
(17e)	"with you away"	[*with* NP XP]	(BE $(x, y_{LOC}))$ CIRCUM COND
(17f)	"with considerable force into our forehead"	[*with* NP PP]	(GO $(x, y_{DIRECTION}))$ CIRCUM COND
(17g)	"with you holding the fort"	[*with* NP VP$_{nonfinite}$]	(V $(x, y))$ CIRCUM COND

8.4.2. Adverbial Phrase Preposing

Observe the sentences in (30).

(30) a. [Never] have I thought of that.

      b. [On the sofa] was John sitting for hours.

      c. [There] goes Mary.

      d. [Away] you go and get turned into a human being.   (*BNC*)

      e. [Away] they flew, across the fields and meadows, over the village and back to Polly's house.   (*BNC*)

      f. [Into Japanese hands] fell Rockefeller Centre in New York, Firestone in Ohio and Columbia Pictures in Hollywood.   (*BNC*)

Chapter 8   The *Dungeon* Construction: A Syntactic Hapax Legomenon   119

g. [Into Tommy's holdall] went the binoculars-camera and the hair curler (one never knew), and I had the cigarette lighter-camera as always in my pocket. *(BNC)*

h. [Into this bizarre vortex] swirls Elizabeth Taylor, whom Andersen depicts as a fatuously verbose and slightly batty Fairy Godmother who waves her wand in all directions to calm Michael's troubles. *(WBO)*

i. [Into this fray of cultural warfare] came feminist journalist Susan Faludi, who published *Backlash: The Undeclared War Against American Women* in October 1991. *(WBO)*

j. [Into the house] she came like an Indiarubber ball, Linda skipping in behind her. *(BNC)*

k. [With Roy away in Quebec], Sulpician Edouard Gagnon, formerly bishop of St Paul, Alberta and now head of the small Canadian College in Rome, was the effective head of the Committee for the Family. *(WBO)*

l. [With any shock into the body] there are only two burns, one where the shock went in and one where it left. *(BNC)*

m. [With the competition now into its full stride], is it time for you to delve into the transfer market?[12] *(WBO)*

In English, there are a variety of adverbial phrases that are preposed. We can prepose a negative phrase in (30a), a locative phrase in (30b), a directional phrase in (30c–j), and a circumstantial conditional phrase in (30k–m). Notice that *away* in (30d, e) is a directional phrase, rather than a locative one. The particle *away* is ambiguous with respect to the semantic type of the main verb. It is either locative as in (31a) or directional as in (32a), but only a directional *away* can prepose. Compare (31b) and (32b):

(31) a.   You are away.

---

[12] Note the sentential nature of this *with*-construction in (30m), with an adverbial *now* inside this construction. It is only because of this clausal nature of the circumstantial conditional *with*-construction that the sentential adverbial *now* could occur quite freely here. Recall the discussion regarding (17d) and (19d).

   Notice that this type of *now* cannot occur in the nonclausal structure [PP *with* NP].

   (i) a. *John is walking along the street {[with *now* Mary]/[with Mary *now*]}.
   b. *John is pushing the cart {[with *now* Mary]/[with Mary *now*]}.

b. *Away you are.

(32) a. You go away.
   b. Away you go.

As far as the process of preposing with regard to the examples in (30) is concerned, we can say that this type of preposing is a major rule since it involves a various types of phrases and a various types of semantic roles. Recall the criterion (12a) in §8.3.2. If there are many types of items that are influenced by a rule R1, for example, then R1 is a major rule, which adverbial preposing is.

8.4.3. Analysis

Let us first look at the examples in (33):

(33) a. Long hours were devoted, lying on the cot in my parents' room, to imagining you kissing me. I was too young, too inexperienced, to contemplate anything beyond that. I accepted the picture, and pasted it into my report, but not before cutting the part [with you away].   (*COCA*)
   b. [With Roy away in Quebec], Sulpician Edouard Gagnon, formerly bishop of St Paul, Alberta and now head of the small Canadian College in Rome, was the effective head of the Committee for the Family. (= (30k))

Clearly, the bracketed parts in (33) are of a *with*-construction of circumstantial conditional interpretation. And there is an important fact about this construction, to which little attention has so far been paid: this type of *with*-construction shows up in the discourse quite independently of the main clause it was supposed to be a part of. Observe (34):

(34) a. After Bill left, Trina cranked up the stereo and continued wallowing in Sondheim albums. She'd never play musicals that loud when Bill was home, nor would he play his jazz albums at a volume that disturbed her. But [**with him away**]... She washed dishes to the thundering Dies Irae chords from Sweeney Todd.
                                          (*COCA*) [Three dots are original‒K.N.]

Chapter 8   The *Dungeon* Construction: A Syntactic Hapax Legomenon   121

b.   # Her stare was fixed on me and terrible. # "It is unimaginable that the neutral mask could be named, say, Zippy, and could wake up in his bed.   [**With you beside him**]." # I can only imagine what I would have said next had she not spoken. # She took off the mask. # "I don't want you to see me," she said. #   (*COCA*)

c.   Republicans are now pinning their hopes of holding the Senate on three states—Missouri, Tennessee and, [**with Ohio off the table**], probably Virginia—while trying to hold on to the House by pouring money into districts where Republicans have a strong historical or registration advantage, party officials said Sunday. (*COCA*)

d.   The opera also would like to add another performance to its three-show runs at the Fox. It can't find the time for that either. Opera productions already tie up the venue for 10 days of dress rehearsal. Then it performs on three of four straight days—Thursday, Saturday and Sunday, [**with Friday off**].   (*COCA*)

e.   "President Nixon sent B-52s over Hanoi for the first time ever. In the next 11 days and nights—[**with Christmas off**]—American planes dropped on North Vietnam 20,000 tons of bombs," amounting to "the explosive equivalent of the Nagasaki A-bomb." (*COCA*)

Now we understand that a circumstantial conditional *with*-construction can stand alone in the discourse. We will focus on certain examples. Let us take (33a) and (34c), for example, and pick out the relevant portions, i.e. the *with*-construction itself, as in (35a, b):

(35) a.   with you away[13]
      b.   with Ohio off the table

Recall that in the previous section, i.e. §8.4.2, we identified adverbial preposing as a major rule. Now, we apply adverbial preposing to (35), and we obtain (36):

(36) a.   Away with you![13]
      b.   Off the table with Ohio!

---

[13] Note that *away* in (35) "with you away" may be Locative, but once preposed, *away* in (36) "Away with you!" is directional. See the discussion regarding the instances in (31) and (32).

Observe that this is the very construction we have ever tried to give a rational, systematic, principled and revealing analysis to. It is the *Dungeon* construction!

Let us give more instances of the construction, including the ones already given in (3). They are shown in (37) below:

(37) a. Into the dungeon with the traitors! (= (3a))
  b. Down with the traitors! (= (3b))
  c. Away with you! (= (3c))
  d. Off with {you / your hat / his head}! (= (3d))
  e. Down the well with your money!
  f. Away with the evidence!   (Jackendoff (1973: 347))
  g. Off with his nose!
  h. Outdoors with these noisy machines!
  i. Upstairs with this illegal card game!

These are indeed the examples of the *Dungeon* construction, and it should be clear that they are an extension from the *with*-construction of the structure [PP *with* NP XP] and that the preposed XPs are all directional phrases.

Now, recall the extension format, once again, which we assumed in §§8.3.1 and 8.3.3. It is repeated below as (38):

(38) If B, then A;
  where B stands for the proposition "the grammar of a language L at stage i (i$\neq$0), G(L, i), has property P'," and A for the proposition "the grammar of the language at the stage i-1, G(L, i-1), has property P." (= (10), (16))

As I stated there, an informal formulation of (38) is as follows: a construction C1 can be extended to another construction C2 if C1, as a forerunner, has a certain set of features that C2 could share. So we ask: What features does the *Dungeon* construction share with the *with*-construction? Before we answer this question, we repeat the peculiar features of the construction that we noted in (7) in §8.2. They are shown in (39) below:

(39) a. It is a nonfinite clause.
  b. It has a directional phrase followed by [PP *with* NP].
  c. NP in the PP [PP *with* NP] is a definite NP.

Chapter 8   The *Dungeon* Construction: A Syntactic Hapax Legomenon   123

d. NP in the PP [PP *with* NP] is the agent/actor or theme of the
    event, or put into syntactic terms, the subject NP in the paraphrase
    for the construction: *the traitors*, for example, in "Into the dun-
    geon with the traitors!" is the agent/actor or theme, or the subject
    NP in the paraphrase "The traitors shall go down into the dun-
    geon!" [Or in a logical representation: (GO (t, d_{GOAL}))]

e. Though the preposition *with* is used to express a whole variety of
    meanings and relations such as 'contact,' 'accompaniment,' 'pos-
    session,' 'instrumental,' 'circumstantial condition,' and many oth-
    ers, it is never followed by an agent/actor or theme, or a subject
    NP. But, note well, so it is only when in the *Dungeon* construc-
    tion. (= (7))

Now it is evidently clear that the *with*-construction that should feed the
Dungeon construction has all the features in (39), except for (39b) since a
with-construction does not have a directional phrase BEFORE [PP *with* NP],
and that it is these features that the *Dungeon* construction shares with the
with-construction. Therefore, we conclude that the *Dungeon* construction is
an extension from the *with*-construction.

8.5.   More on the *Dungeon* Construction: Further Extension

It has been a longstanding question in the inquiries of Grammatical
Dynamism to ask how far extension goes or, in other words, when it stops. In
the extension format (38) in the previous section, there is no point, by definition, where we can prevent the process from progressing further forward.
And, indeed, it is the case with the *with*-construction. Extension goes a step
farther. Observe (40):

(40) a. Get along with you, and go to bed.   (*OED*, s.v. *with* (prep.))
     b. Get along with you, vagrant!   (*COCA*)
     c. Go along with you!   (*OED*, s.v. *with* (prep.), *go* (v.))
     d. Now go along with you. Try to come back with a smile on your
         face. It troubles me to see you looking so lost. (2009)   (*COHA*)
     e. Get away with you, young Tamborel!   (*COCA*)

124   *A Dynamic Study of Some Derivative Processes in English Grammar*

These are definitely the *Dungeon* construction, and they do differ from the examples in (41) below in that *you*'s and *your belongings* in (41), i.e. NPs after *with*, all mean accompaniment, but never assume the subject/agent/theme function.

(41) a. They will get along with you.
   b. They will go along with you.
   c. Get away with your belongings.

   The next question we may ask is: How can we arrive at examples like those in (40)? At first it might seem plausible to derive those in (40) from the ones in (42), by preposing *get along*, *go along* and *get away*, respectively:

(42) a. *[*with* you get along]
   b. *[*with* you go along].
   c. *[*with* you get away].

But the problem with this approach is the fact that the underlying structures in (42) are all wrong. But the reality is that examples in (40) are all right. How can we get out of this difficult situation?   There is the extension format. Observe the *Dungeon* construction we gave in (37) in the previous section, which we repeat below:

(37) a. Into the dungeon with the traitors! (= (3a))
   b. Down with the traitors! (= (3b))
   c. Away with you! (= (3c))
   d. Off with {you/your hat/his head}! (= (3d))
   e. Down the well with your money!
   f. Away with the evidence!   (Jackendoff (1973: 347))
   g. Off with his nose!
   h. Outdoors with these noisy machines!
   i. Upstairs with this illegal card game!

The *Dungeon* construction in (37) has, among others, one important feature as represented in (43):

(43)   [DIRECTIONAL PHRASE XP] [*with* NP$_{\text{SUBJECT/AGENT/THEME}}$]!

And the structure of (40a), for example, is (44):

Chapter 8   The *Dungeon* Construction: A Syntactic Hapax Legomenon   125

(44)   [DIRECTIONAL PHRASE [VPnonfinite get along]] [*with* youSUBJECT/AGENT/
THEME]!

It has been repeatedly claimed that the 'small clause' in the *with*-construction
is nonfinite, as exemplified in (45), and it is notably this nonfiniteness that examples in (40) inherited.

(45)   You didn't have to cook after your day's work, which has to be
heavier [with [Frank away] and [you holding the fort]]. (= (17g))

In (45), nonfiniteness is guaranteed by the participle ending in *holding*, and in
(44) it is also guaranteed by the infinitive form of *get*. Next, how is it the
case that we can claim that *get along* in (44) is directional? The answer is: the
phrase "get along" necessarily implies movement such as 'GO FROM X TO
Y' and, therefore, it surely stands for the phrase of direction.

Therefore, our analysis is that the *Dungeon* construction has a set of features, and it is these features that the extended *Dungeon* construction (40)
shares with the *Dungeon* construction (37), the latter being the basic type and
the former the derivative type.

8.6.   Conclusion

We have made a certain approach to the *Dungeon* construction, and also
to its extended construction, and made it clear that there exists an extension
process in the grammar of English that is guided by a principle in Linguistic
Theory, i.e. the extension format. Only through this approach, we believe, the
analysis of the *Dungeon* construction is made possible; all other approaches
can't seem to accommodate the strange construction with all its intriguing
properties.[14] This fact confirms our extension format in Grammatical
Dynamism.

The *Dungeon* construction (37) itself is a result of construction extension,
i.e. it is a derived construction, and the extended *Dungeon* construction (40) is
a further derived one. As far as I can see, there is no further extension of this

---

[14] The *can't seem to* construction may plausibly be called another syntactic hapax legomenon. See Langendoen (1970), Kajita (1974: 429) and the last paragraph of this section.

type of construction in the grammar of English. So the rules responsible for the *Dungeon* construction are minor rules. There is such a term as 'hapax legomenon' in the literature. A hapax legomenon is "a word or form evidenced by a single citation: a word or form occurring once and only in a document or corpus." (*Webster*[3]) With all this in mind, we may call the *Dungeon* construction as a whole a syntactic hapax legomenon.

PART III

Dynamic Model Reviewed and Revised: Theoretical Issues

In Part III, we point out that there are some puzzles, both empirical and theoretical, in Kajita's (2002) formulation of Grammatical Dynamism, which we observed in §8.3.1. We will see what the puzzles are, propose a revised format, and give evidence for the revised model in the subsequent chapters.

Chapter 9

Empirical Puzzles

9.1. Grammatical Dynamism

Grammatical Dynamism, or Dynamic Model, is a theory of grammar advocated by Kajita (1977, 1997, 2002, and elsewhere) claiming that as children acquire language in the step-by-step mode, so the grammar of a human language be constructed in the brain of a child in the same mode. Thus, while Chomsky's (1965, 1995, 2013, and elsewhere) approach does not in principle refer to the intermediate stages between the initial and final state of grammar, Grammatical Dynamism refers to each of the stages of grammatical development. So the former is often called an output-oriented theory, and the latter a process-oriented theory. In other words, the former considers that language acquisition can theoretically be made possible instantaneously, but the latter proposes that it needs to refer to the intermediate stages. So the former is also called an instantaneous or static model, while the latter a dynamic model. See §8.3.1 of chapter 8 for the references and the details of Grammatical Dynamism.

Kajita's formulation of the process of extension has often been referred to in the previous chapters. Once again I repeat it here:

(1) If the grammar of a language L at stage i, G(L, i), has property P,

128

then the grammar of the language at the next stage, G(L, i+1), may have property P′. 　　　　　　　　　　　　　　　(Kajita (2002: 161))

As I noted in §8.3.1 of chapter 8, the formulation of (1) can be rephrased in an abstract form as in (2), where A stands for the proposition "the grammar of a language L at stage i, G(L, i), has property P," and B for the proposition "the grammar of the language at the next stage, G(L, i+1), has property P′."

(2)　If A, then B is possible.

In the following sections of this chapter, we note a number of empirical puzzles that arise from the formulation of (2).

9.2.　Possible but Nonexistent Examples: Accidental Gaps

There are cases where one certain example is structurally approvable in the sense that it is in accordance with the grammatical rules of the language, but in reality it is ungrammatical. In other words, there are accidental gaps in the language.

In chapter 2, we noted such examples as in (3):

(3)　Problem 1: *decímeter, *centímeter *millímeter
　　　Problem 2: *sálimèter
　　　Problem 3: *myriámeter
　　　Problem 4: *báromèter, *clínomèter, *ódomèter, *táchomèter, *thérmomèter

Words in (3) are expected to be grammatical, but they are not. In chapter 3, we noted such examples as in (4)–(6):

(4)　a.　compúlsive
　　　b.　compúlsory
　　　c.　úlcer

(5)　a.　expúlse—expúlsion
　　　b.　ímpùlse—impúlsion
　　　c.　repúlse—repúlsion

(6) a.   filth—filthy
    b.   héalth—héalthy
    c.   wéalth—wéalthy

Words in (4) are expected to have [lts] in them, but they lack it. All words in (5) are expected to have excrescent [t] in them, but the fact is such that while the left-hand words have [lts], the right-hand ones fail to have *[ltʃ]. In (6), while the left-hand words are expected to have [ltθ] in them and indeed they do have [ltθ], the right-hand words, contrary to our expectation, lack it. In chapter 4, we noted that there is a phenomenon I call Grammatical Naturalization, an example of which is (7a) turned (7b). Notice that (8b) should also be grammatical because of the structural parallelism between (7) and (8). But the fact is (8b) is wrong.

(7) a.   John drank a cup of tea quickly.
    b.   Joh drank a quick cup of tea.

(8) a.   John served a cup of tea quickly.
    b.   *John served a quick cup of tea.

In chapter 6, we noted that there is a head-internal relative clause (HIRC) construction in English, such as the one in (9):

(9)   The closest anyone came to him was the man who leaned over.

This means that we have a clause introducer of the form [*the* + Superlative] in English HIRC, but the superlative is exclusively limited to *closest* and *nearest*, and no other, as far as I have investigated.

According to the format of (1) and (2) in §9.1, the above examples that are supposed to be fine should be fine, but in reality while there are some that are fine, there are others that are not. We cannot tell which is fine and which is bad. In other words, we cannot generate grammatical sequences and only these.

9.3.   Improbable but Existent Examples: Accidental Haps

In general, we do not expect an example to exist in the language such that it has a set of features that have eventually escaped linguists' and gram-

Chapter 9 Empirical Puzzles 131

marians' eyes, or that it will simply be judged ungrammatical by almost all linguists and grammarians. But, in reality, there exists such an example. When there is something that we believe to exist but in fact there is no such a thing, we call it an accidental gap. By the similar fashion, let us call the case of improbable but existent examples an accidental hap. And we know there is no small number of accidental haps in English.

In chapter 4, we noted such an example as in (10):

(10)   Sam kicked the *proverbial* bucket.   (Chafe (1968: 124))

The idiom "to kick the bucket," with its uncompositional meaning 'to die,' is one of the most recalcitrant types of idioms. Adjectives are not allowed in this idiom under the idiomatic reading, as shown in (11):

(11) a. *John kicked the white bucket.
      b. *John kicked the small bucket.
      c. *John kicked the wooden bucket.

But as we see in (10), an adjective *proverbial* easily slides into the heart of the 'frozen' idiom. So we may call (10) an accidental hap. In chapter 6, we observed that there exist HIRCs in English. No linguist has ever referred to the existence of the English HIRC, let alone an analysis of it. But as we saw in chapter 6, the example in (12) below is a sentence with a HIRC in the subject position.

(12)   The closest anyone came to him was the man who leaned over.

Thus English HIRC is an accidental hap. In chapter 8, we explicated the entangled nature of the *Dungeon* construction, an example of which is given in (13):

(13)   Into the dungeon with the traitors!

We cannot expect a preposition *with* to have an NP that follows that assumes a subject function or an agent / theme role. But the fact is that the NP *the traitors* in (13) does assume a subject function and an agent / theme role. Thus the example in (13) is an accidental hap.

In the formulation of extension in (1) and (2), we cannot explain the existence of accidental haps. In my view, the reason is as follows. In the formulation of (1), for example, we do not have as part of property P the statement such that the idiom "to kick the bucket" allows an adjective to occur inside the NP *the bucket*. Given this condition in the antecedent of (1), how can we expect such a statement that the idiom "to kick the bucket" allows an adjective to occur inside the NP *the bucket*, as part of property P′ in the consequent of (1)? The answer is, it seems to me, we cannot: this is equivalent to saying, in a grossly simplified form, that if we do not have X, then we may have X.

The same line of argument applies to other accidental haps. Therefore, it is concluded that the format in (1) and (2) induces empirical puzzles.

Chapter 10

Theoretical Puzzles

In the following sections of this chapter, we note a number of theoretical puzzles that arise from the formulation of (1) and (2) in §9.1 in chapter 9.

10.1. How Far Extension Goes and When to Stop

Let us repeat below the extension format in §9.1 in chapter 9:

(1) If the grammar of a language L at stage i, G(L, i), has property P, then the grammar of the language at the next stage, G(L, i+1), may have property P'.   (Kajita (2002: 161))

(2) If A, then B is possible;
where A stands for the proposition "the grammar of a language L at stage i, G(L, i), has property P," and B for the proposition "the grammar of the language at the next stage, G(L, i+1), has property P'."

As we observed in chapter 9, there are accidental gaps (§9.2) and accidental haps (§9.3) in English. Accidental gaps are the cases where we expect a lot more but we do not have any more. Accidental haps are the cases where we do not want any more but we do have some more. Empirical examples are drawn from the cases of stress assignment of -*meter* words, occurrence of ex-

133

134   *A Dynamic Study of Some Derivative Processes in English Grammar*

crescent [t], Grammatical Naturalization (or transferred epithet), English HIRCs and the *Dungeon* construction. From a logical point of view, (1) and (2) simply tell us that there is a possibility of extension, but no more. As far as extension is concerned, there is no account as to how far it goes and when it stops. This is a theoretical puzzle.

10.2. Grammatical Roudabout or Else

In§7.6 in chapter 7, we noted the following:

[Begins quotation #1]
But consider the vowel [ʌ] in *money*. The vowel is just asking for trouble if, instead of remaining as it is, it circumvents the easiest goal and takes the longer way to the other goal.

(31)   money [mʌni]

(32)   monetize [mʌnətaiz]

(33)   monetize [manətaiz]

What I mean is that it should be much easier for (31) to arrive at (32) than it is for (31) to arrive at (33). Thus (31) is least motivated to arrive at (33), but this is what actually happens. Or consider the Grammatically Naturalized adjectives, which are discussed in the last section [§7.5.2]. They have the least motivation to arrive at the place where they have no semantic relationship around there. But this is what actually happens. [...]

   Or if the current rigorous formal linguists' theories are output-oriented theories, as Kajita terms them in Kajita (1997, 2001, and elsewhere), we wonder why (31) has an exceptional vowel [ʌ]. For, if (31) had the regular vowel [a], it could directly arrive at the output state of (33). But the reality is that (31) has the irregular vowel [ʌ]. Or if output-oriented theorists say that having the vowel [a] is the output condition for the letter -o- with a primary stress on it, then what should we do with the examples in (16) and (18)? [(16): abóve, cóme, cómfort, etc., (18): accómpany, cómfortable, hóneymoon, etc.]

   Furthermore, if output theorists are correct, we wonder why

Chapter 10   Theoretical Puzzles   135

Grammatically Naturalized adjectives step into the slots where semantic consistency is outlawed. The output state should have guaranteed the semantic consistency, but, as we can see, the result is catastrophically inconsistant from a semantic point of view.

So the process-oriented theories, as Kajita's terminology goes, seem promising. Process-oriented theories dictate the possible transitions from one state to the next. The exceptional vowel [ʌ] in (31) will find, in the next stage, the regular vowel [ɑ] as the possible vowel for the letter -o- with a primary stress on it. And as for the cases of Grammatical Naturalization, it seems likely that once the sentential / VP adverbial has been turned into an adjective, this adjective will find the prenominal position as the best possible site for her in the next step of derivation, because [Det A N] is the most standard and prevalent nominal sturucture in English.
[End of quotation #1]

Now it is clear that there are cases where a certain process of extension is counter-intuitive. In the case of *money* and *monetize*, the process of vowel alteration is literally 'far-fetched,' or in plain English, it takes a longer, roundabout way to the goal. It is counter-economical, which is in effect counterintuitive.

Next, the case of Grammatical Naturalization. Contrary to what I wrote in the last paragraph of the quotation #1, I understand, from the vantage point here in this context, that it is rather hard for us to analyze Grammatical Naturalization in line with the formulation of (1) and (2). The reason is, as I wrote in §9.3 in chapter 9, like this:

[Begins quotation #2]
In the formulation of (1), for example, we do not have as part of property P the statement such that the idiom "to kick the bucket" allows an adjective to occur inside the NP *the bucket*. Given this condition in the antecedent of (1), how can we expect such a statement that the idiom "to kick the bucket" allows an adjective to occur inside the NP *the bucket*, as part of property P′ in the consequent of (1)? The answer is, it seems to me, we cannot: this is equivalent to saying, in a grossly simplified form, that if we do not have X, then we may have X.
[End of quotation #2]

Or, to take another perspective, the statement in (3) below, which is in the last paragraph of the quotation #1, appears to be on shaky ground.

(3) ..., it seems likely that once the sentential / VP adverbial has been turned into an adjective, this adjective will find the prenominal position as the best possible site for her in the next step of derivation, ...

That is, where does the proposition "once the sentential / VP adverbial has been turned into an adjective" belong in the formulation of (1)? If it belongs in P, this means that Grammatical Naturalization is almost finished at stage i. There is no need to refer to the extension format. If it belongs in P′, then what kind of motivation can we expect at stage i in order to realize this syntactic category changing at the next stage i+1? We know that there is a category changing rule of this type in the lexicon, or in the word formation component, but here in this case we need a category changing rule of this type at the level of syntax, which, by supposition, is stated in P′. In short, what is it that there is at stage i that motivates this category changing "Adv → Adj," quite independently of Grammatical Naturalization? At present, I can think of no reasonable answer to this.

Therefore, it seems appropriate to conclude that the formulation of (1) and (2) leads us to a roubabout or else somewhere near what we might call impasse in the theoretical perspective.

10.3. Tautology

The most serious concern about the formulation (1) will come out in a clearer form in (2), which is repeated below:

(2) If A, then B is possible;
where A stands for the proposition "the grammar of a language L at stage i, G(L, i), has property P," and B for the proposition "the grammar of the language at the next stage, G(L, i+1), has property P′."

The formulation (2) can be paraphrased as in (4), with the provision after *where* suppressed:

(4) If A, then B or ~B.

Now, let us make a truth functional table for this proposition (4).

Table 1: Truth Functional Table for (4)

A	B	~B	B or ~B	If A, then B or ~B.
T	T	F	T	T
T	F	T	T	T
F	T	F	T	T
F	F	T	T	T

No matter what truth value A and B may have (T or F), the proposition "If A, then B or ~B" always comes out as T. This means that the format (1), and of course (2), is a tautology. As an instance of tautology, (1) is always true whatever properties P and P′ may have. For example, as part of P, we may have "all consonants are implosives," and as part of P′ "the 25th consonant from the beginning of a sentence is replaced by the glottal stop when the sentence is a question asked by a person in his/her sixties." Still, this proposition comes out true. (Cf. note 2 of chapter 11.)

In general, linguistics is regarded as an empirical science, and an empirical science needs to face empirical facts in the course of research. But in the case of (1) and (2), you do not need to see facts for the entire proposition to be true. No matter how strange, awkward, absurd and least factual the statement in P or P′ may be, the proposition (1), and of course (2), will always be true. Being a tautology, the formuation of (1), and needless to say (2), is not a desired one as a statement in empirical science.

Chapter 11

The Revised Dynamic Model

11.1. Dynamic Model Revised

In chapters 9 and 10, we have seen many puzzles that are ascribed to the formulation of (1) and its abstract counterpart (2). (1) and (2) of chapters 9 and 10 are repeated below:

(1) If the grammar of a language L at stage i, G(L, i), has property P, then the grammar of the language at the next stage, G(L, i+1), may have property P'. (Kajita (2002: 161))

(2) If A, then B is possible;
where A stands for the proposition "the grammar of a language L at stage i, G(L, i), has property P," and B for the proposition "the grammar of the language at the next stage, G(L, i+1), has property P'."

We propose that (1) and (2) be revised as (3), and if we informally restate (3), it will be something like (4):

(3) The Revised Extension Format
If B, then A;
where B stands for the proposition "the grammar of a language L at stage i (i≠0), G(L, i), has property P'," and A for the proposition "the

138

Chapter 11   The Revised Dynamic Model   139

grammar of the language at the stage i-1, G(L, i-1), has property P."

(4)   If we have a property P′ in the grammar G′ at a certain stage, then we have as a forerunner a property P in the grammar G before that stage.

The significant departure of (3) from (1) and (2) is in the order of appearance of A and B. At first, you might be tempted to say that in (2), A is a sufficient condition, and B a necessary condition. But (2) can be paraphrased as (5) below:

(5)   Either "If A, then B" or "If A, then ~B."

Informally stated, (5) means this: in a representation in the form of Venn diagram, B is properly included in A. This in turn means (6):

(6)   If B, then A.

So, contrary to our first impression of the appearance of (2), we say A is a necessary condition and B a sufficient condition even in (2). But this only means the logical equivalence between (2) and (3). Empirically speaking, (2) still differs from (3). So what is the difference? Why is the formulation of (3) proposed over that of (2)? In the next chapter, i.e. chapter 12, we will be concerned with the significance of the formulation (3).

Some words are in order here as regards the logic about the interpretation of (1) and (2) above. There may be arguments against the discussion that concludes that in (2), A is a necessary condition and B a sufficient condition.[1] I will tentatively say that the latter coclusion results from a 'loose' interpretation of the conditional "If A, then B is possible." Namely, the interpretation such that B is properly included in A, in Venn diagram. However, there is another interpretation, which I will call a 'strict' intrerpretation. According to the 'strict' interpretation, it is implausible to conclude that "If A, then B is possible" can be paraphrased as "If B, then A": "If A, then B is possible" is simply "If A, then B or ~B" and no more.[2] If we take the 'strict' interpretation view, it is not the case that (2) and (3) are logically equivalent. And, of

---

[1] Due to Eric McCready (personal communication).

[2] If this is the case, the consequent, i.e. "B or ~B", means a universe U in Venn diagram. In this case, "If A, then B is possible" means that A is always included in U.

course, (2) empirically differs from (3). Therefore, regardless of the interpretation of the conditional "If A, then B is possible," whether 'loose' or 'strict,' it is the case that (2) empirically differs from (3). So what is the difference? Why is the formulation of (3) proposed over that of (2)? In the next chapter, we are concerned with the significance of the formulation (3).

We propose, in addtion to (3), a mode of extension, which we often referred to in the previous chapters, i.e. chapters 3–5.

(7)   Mode of Extension
    a.   TYPE A
        If an item a of the category X is in the structure S, then another item b of the same category X is in the structure S.
    b.   TYPE B
        If an item a of the category X is in the structure S, then an item b of the category X' is in the structure S, where b in X' is the counterpart of a in X.

The mode of extension in (7) is of course guided by the principle of the extension format (3) above. It plays an important role in many analyses in Part II, and it is especially notable that it does so in the analysis of poetic interpretation of Keats' *To Autumn* in chapter 5.

Chapter 12

Evidence for the Revised Model

12.1. Significance of the Revised Model

12.1.1. Empirical Puzzles Overcome

In chapter 9 we noted two types of empirical puzzles: possible but non-existent cases (accidental gaps) and improbable but existent ones (accidental haps). Now look again at the revised extension format and its informal formulation in chapter 11, which are repeated below:

(1) The Revised Extension Format
If B, then A;
where B stands for the proposition "the grammar of a language L at stage i (i≠0), G(L, i), has property P'," and A for the proposition "the grammar of the language at the stage i-1, G(L, i-1), has property P."

(2) If we have a property P' in the grammar G' at a certain stage, then we have as a forerunner a property P in the grammar G before that stage.

It shoul be clear that since nonexistent cases are simply the cases that do not exist, they are not the target of linguistic description. The extension format just says things about existing objets. Observe closely the formulation of (1) and (2). Notice, in this connection, that empirical theories only claim that there exist such and such objects in the empirical world, but says nothing about nonexisting objects. We analyze a certain linguistic phenomenon and give a detailed structural description to it, so we virtually know that nonexistent examples are the ones that failed to meet this structural description. But, once again, theories say nothing about the nonexistent objects. Therefore, we have no problem concerning accidental gaps.

Now, how about accidental haps? Our revised model goes this way. If we have as part of P′ in the antecedent of (1) and (2) the statement that the idiom "to kick the bucket" allows an adjective to occur inside the NP *the bucket*, then we have all the analyais given inchapter 4, an analysis on Grammatical Naturalization, as part of P in the consequent of (1) and (2). Similarly, if we have as part of P′ in the antecedent of (1) and (2) the statement about the existence of English HIRCs, then we have all the analysis on English HIRCs given in chapter 6, as part of P in the consequent of (1) and (2). And if we have as part of P′ in the antecedent of (1) and (2) the statement about the peculiar features of the *Dungeon* construction, then we have all the analysis on the *Dungeon* construction given in chapter 8, as part of P in the consequent of (1) and (2).

Therefore, we no longer have the kind of empirical puzzles we have if we accepted the 'old' extension format.

12.1.2. Theoretical Puzzles Overcome

In chapter 10 we noted three types of theoretical puzzles: puzzles concerning (i) how far extension goes and when to stop, (ii) grammatical roundabout and related issues, and (iii) tautology.

Fisrt of all, regarding the puzzle (i), let us note that we have such a wording as "may" and "possible" in the 'old' format of extension, as we can see, e.g., in (1) and (2) of §11.1 in chapter 11. But now, we do not have such a wording in the revised format. Essentially, the puzzle of "how far extension goes and when to stop" entirely depends on the existence of the notion 'possibility,' the wording of "may" and "possible" being embodiment of this notion. Once the 'old' format says "B is possible," it entails that there is either B or ~B. This statement inevitably invites the question (3a). And the answer should be (3b):

(3) a. What is it that discerns B and ~B, or when is it that there is B and there isn't B?

b. It just happens, and when it doesn't, it doesn't.

This means that the 'old' format cannot EXPLAIN the accidental existence on the logical basis. The revised format, however, employs no wording like "may" or "possible," but even without this wording, it implies the very notion 'possibility' quite successfully. Let us illustrate this.

In the revised extension format of (1) in §12.1.1 (i.e. "if B, then A"), let us suppose it is also the case that "if B′, then A." Suppose further that in reality it is never the case that B′ is true (i.e. the case of accidental gap). In this case, you might ask (4a). Our answer is simple: it is (4b):

(4) a. Why is B′ empirically not true?

b. Because there does not exist the case where B′ is true.

On the face of it, (3b) and (4b) might look alike, but they are logically distinct. (3b) is an answer to an inevitable question that has to be answered. And as an answer itself, (3b) is not an 'answer': a totally unsatisfactory 'answer.' But in the case of (4b), the question that invites the answer (4b) is not an inevitable one. It just pops up without any necessity. And the answer (4b) is fine by itself: it means that there does not exist the case where B′ is true only by chance. Here, note well the phrase "only by chance." Now, it is clear that even without the wording of "possibility" and the like in the revised format, this revised format implies the very notion 'possibility' quite successfully. No logical convolution involved here.

Next, we take up the puzzles regarding (ii), i.e. those about the grammatical roundabout and related issues. Let us take the example of *money* and *monetize*. Our analysis goes as follows. In the revised format (1) in §12.1.1, we have as part of P′ the statement (5a) and as part of P the statement (5b):

(5) a. As part of P′: The word *money* has a short stressed vowel [ʌ] for the letter -*o*-; the word *monetize* has a short stressed vowel [ɑ] for the letter -*o*-.

b. As part of P: The word *money* has a short stressed vowel [ʌ] for the letter -*o*-; according to the normal sound-spelling relationship in English, when the letter -o- represents a short stressed vowel, it is [ɑ].

Now it is clear that *monetize* with a short stressed vowel [ɑ] is a normal practice. And since in P there are two descriptions such as, first, a descritption about *money* with a short stressed vowel [ʌ] and, second, a description about the normal practice of a letter -o- having a short stressed vowel [ɑ], we know that in the case of *money* having the vowel [ʌ], it is an exceptional feature for the word *money* to have a vowel [ʌ] in the place of the letter -o-. There is no roundabout here.

How about the case of Grammatical Naturalization? In the revised format (1) in §12.1.1, we have as part of P′ the statement (6a) and as part of P the statement (6b):

(6) a. As part of P′: The idiom "to kick the bucket" allows an adjective to occur inside the NP *the bucket*.

b. As part of P: All the analysis in chapter 4.

It is straightforward. There is no impasse here, either.

Finally, let us look at the third puzzle (iii) tautology. Clearly, the revised extension format (1) in §12.1.1 is no longer a tautology. See below the truth functional table for (1):

Table 1: Truth Functional Table for (1)

B	A	If B, then A.
T	T	T
T	F	F
F	T	T
F	F	T

The table 1 itself is sufficient to show that the proposition is something other than tautology. But let me give an illustration. For example, if we have as part of P′ the statement (7a) and as part of P the statement (7b), the entire proposition "If B, then A" comes out as F. Thus it is falsifiable.

(7) a. As part of P′: The preposition *with* in the *Dungeon* construction is followed by a subject NP or agent / theme NP.

b. As part of P: The preposition *with* is followed by an NP with such

Chapter 12   Evidence for the Revised Model   145

a semantic role as commitative, instrumental, and possessive, but no other.

But if we replace (7b) by (7c) below, the proposition becomes true.

(7) c.   As part of P: All the analysis of chapter 8, including "the preposition *with* is followed by an NP with such a semantic role as commitative, instrumental, possessive, agent and theme."

The act of replacing (7b) by (7c) is in fact a process of our endeavor to analyze the *Dungeon* construction.

Empirical science needs to do research directly related to a variety of types of empirical facts so that it has to be falsifiable. Since our revised extension format is fully falsifiable, it is part of empirical science.

12.2.   More on the Revised Extension Format

Supppose, for ease of exposition, that we have three stages in the development of an adult grammar, G_1, G_2 and G_3. Suppose further that there is a feature f in each of the properties P^1, P^2 and P^3 that belong to G_1, G_2 and G_3, respectively. In other words, f is consitently present in the development of an adult grammar. In the cases like this, we often say that a basic feature survives a long way, or that what is learned in the early days remain for a long time. From the perspective of our revised extension format, we name the feature f a basic feature, but not the other way around. That is, it is not the case that first, there is an a priori basic feature, and then this feature survives. The real interpretation is: what remained until the last stage is sometimes called a 'basic' feature.

12.3.   Simple Illustration of the Adequacy of the Revised Model

Let us illustrate the adequacy of the revised model of (1) in §12.1.1, taking as examples some daily issues around us. To do this, we employ the informal version (2), and modify it slightly, as shown in (8) below:

(8)   If there is a property P' in the human H' at a certain stage, then there

146   *A Dynamic Study of Some Derivative Processes in English Grammar*

is as a forerunner a property P in the human H before that stage.

Suppose we have as part of P′ the statement (9a) and as part of P the statement (9b):

(9) a. As part of P′: John is twenty years old on January 1, 2015.

b. As part of P: John is nineteen years old on January 1, 2014.

Now, the entire proposition "If B, then A," which is the abstract form of (8), is true. But what if we have (9c) or (9d) as part of P?

(9) c. As part of P: John is ten years old on January 1, 2014.

d. As part of P: John is thirty years old on January 1, 2015.

It is easy to see that the entire proposition "If B, then A" is false. Thus the revised model is falsifiable.

Consider, on the other hand, what the 'old' model implies. The 'old' format will have an informal version like (10):

(10) If there is a property P in the human H at a certain stage, then there is either a property P′ or a property ~P′ in the human H′ after that stage.

The abstract form of (10) is "If A, then B or ~B." Let us look at the truth functional table for this proposition. Here, we suppose that (9a) and (9b) are true and that (9c) and (9d) are false.

Table 2: Truth Functional Table for (10)

A	B	~B	B or ~B	If A, then B or ~B.
(9b) = T	(9a) = T	F	T	T
(9c) = F	(9a) = T	F	T	T
(9d) = F	(9a) = T	F	T	T

Now we can see that the 'old' model implies that everything goes: whatever age John may be on January 1, 2014 or on January 1, 2015, the entire proposition always comes out as true. This is counter-intuitive, or, we should say, counter-empirical. This is the tautological nature of the 'old' model. Thus the 'old' model lacks falsifiability while the revised model satisfies it.

12.4. The Nature of Logical Implication

It is worth noting that the logical implication of the form "If X, then Y" is nothing but a logical relation between X and Y, and that it has nothing to do with such a temporal-sequential notion that "First X happens, and then Y subsequently happens." Thus the logical implication "If X, then Y" is independent of time reference. This is evidently clear in the simple case of "If John is twenty years old on January 1, 2015, then John is nineteen years old on January 1, 2014," an example of the previous section. Independence of time reference applies to our revised model as well. Our model, i.e. (1) in §12.1.1 below, is justifiably in line with this nature of logical implication.

(1) The Revised Extension Format

If B, then A;

where B stands for the proposition "the grammar of a language L at stage i (i≠0), G(L, i), has property P'," and A for the proposition "the grammar of the language at the stage i-1, G(L, i-1), has property P."

(1) just says that there is a logical implicational relation between B and A and no more. (1) never claims that B happens first, and then A happens subsequently.

From a perspective of language acquisition, the format (1) simply claims that a child at the stage i-1 can acquire ANY grammar that is compatible with the format (1) at the next stage i. It is a ceaseless effort on the part of linguists to identify the features, crystalize the regularities, and formulate all these characteristics, of P' and P in an explicit and falsifiable manner.

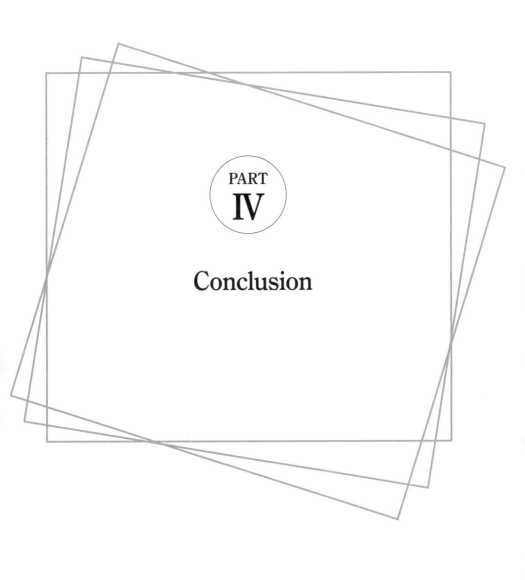

PART IV

Conclusion

Chapter 13

Towards a Theory of Explanation

13.1. The Revised Extension Format as an Explanatory Theory

In Part III, we have shown the significance of our revised extension format. The format is in (1) and its informal formulation in (2):

(1) The Revised Extension Format
If B, then A;
where B stands for the proposition "the grammar of a language L at stage i (i≠0), G(L, i), has property P′," and A for the proposition "the grammar of the language at the stage i-1, G(L, i-1), has property P."

(2) If we have a property P′ in the grammar G′ at a certain stage, then we have as a forerunner a property P in the grammar G before that stage.

As I discussed in detail there, the 'old' format has a number of puzzles that have to be solved. But as far as I can see, we can't seem to solve them. So I proposed (1), and its informal version (2). The revised format accommodates the puzzles the 'old' one failed to, and furthermore, from a logical point of view, it is no longer a tautology.

The revised format is a most abstract statement in linguistic research. So

Chapter 13   Towards a Theory of Explanation   151

it should be on the level of Linguistic Theory, which we referred to in chapter
1. Now, recall the notion "explanation" that I touched upon in §1.2 in chapter
1. When Linguistic Theory rules the behavior of English Grammar, we say
Linguistic Theory explains English Grammar. Then we may ask: What is explained in English Grammar? The answer is the manner of explanation such
that English Grammar obeys the format of (1). Then we may ask: What is
explained in the English Language? The answer is, again, the manner of explanation. For a better view of the latter explanation, let us give an illustration. In fact, we have already seen the 'explanation relationship' between
Grammar and Language, for example, in §12.1.2. Let me repeat the examples
of (5)–(7) there, below:

(3) a.   As part of P′: The word *money* has a short stressed vowel [ʌ] for
the letter *-o-*; the word *monetize* has a short stressed vowel [ɑ] for
the letter *-o-*.

   b.   As part of P: The word *money* has a short stressed vowel [ʌ] for
the letter *-o-*; according to the normal sound-spelling relationship
in English, when the letter *-o-* represents a short stressed vowel, it
is [ɑ]. (= (§12.1.2 (5)))

(4) a.   As part of P′: The idiom "to kick the bucket" allows an adjective
to occur inside the NP *the bucket*.

   b.   As part of P: All the analysis in chapter 4. (= (§12.1.2 (6)))

(5) a.   As part of P′: The preposition *with* in the *Dungeon* construction is
followed by a subject NP or agent / theme NP.

   b.   As part of P: The preposition *with* is followed by an NP with such
a semantic role as commitative, instrumental, and possessive, but
no other.

   c.   As part of P: All the analysis of chapter 8, including "the preposition
with is followed by an NP with such a semantic role as commitative,
instrumental, possessive, agent and theme." (= (§12.1.2 (7)))

Notice that (5b) is a false proposition, so we disregard it. In general, the
statement in P′ includes description about facts, and the statement in P the
structural description about these facts. This is the relationship that Linguistic
Theory, in particular the revised format (1), dictates. This is what we call
'explanation.'

The revised format (1) also explains accidental gaps and accidental haps, i.e. the question of "why this form but not that one?" This is what we call 'a higher order of explanation.' Cf. §1.2.2. In other words, the revised format (1) is successful in explaining both the empirical and the theoretical puzzles that would surface if we assumed the 'old' format.

13.2. Summary

In this thesis, I investigated some derivative processes observed in English, thereby providing analyses of these 'constructions,' which constitute part of English Grammar. I then stepped forward to the question of "why this form but not that one?" This consideration has led us to a proposal that should be stated in Linguistic Theory. On the way to this goal, I assumed Grammatical Dynamism advocated by Kajita (1977, 1997, 2002, and elsewhere), and revised it so as to be a falsifiable model. If the revision is on the right track, it is hoped that it will pave the way towards linguistic explanation that many a linguist has ever sought and wished for.

Finally, I should note that we add a provision to the revised format of (1) and (2):

(6) Provision to the Revised Format (1) and (2)
     P′ and P share at least a certain set of features.

The importance of this provision is evidenced in the analyses of Part II and in the discussion of Part III. A formal formulation of this 'sharing-features' requirement is given in the chapters 3 through 5 in the form of "Mode of Extension." Just as this provision is important, it is also necessarily essential, it seems to me, as far as (1), and of course (2), aims to be part of the hypothesis that deals with empirical fields like linguistics. Otherwise, the model of (1) and (2) would be able to handle the situations where descriptions of P′ and P are totally unrelated with each other. And the model could even accommodate such unworldly matters that belong to fictitious possible worlds.[1] Thus (6) is a necessary provision in the theory of Grammatical Dynamism.

---

[1] See, for example, the discussions about conditionals found in McCawley (1993) and Jackson (1991). I am indebted to Eric McCready for directing my attention to the latter volume.

References

Dictionaries

The Concise Oxford Dictionary, Tenth Edition, (1999) Oxford University Press, Oxford. [*COD*]

The Kenkyusha Dictionary of English Philology, (1940) ed. by Sanki Ichikawa, Kenkyusha, Tokyo.

The Oxford English Dictionary, Second Edition, (1989) Oxford University Press, Oxford. [*OED*]

Random House Unabridged Dictionary, Second Edition, (1993 edition) Random House, New York. [*RHD^2*] [*Random House Unabridged Dictionary, Second Edition,* is a revised and updated edition of *The Random House Dictionary of the English Language, Second Edition, Unabridged.*]

Random House Webster's College Dictionary, (1991 edition) Random House, New York. [*RHW*]

Webster's New World Dictionary of American English, Third College Edition, (1988 edition) Webster's New World, New York. [*WNW*]

Webster's Ninth New Collegiate Dictionary, Merriam-Webster, Springfield, MA. (1987) [*WNNCD*]

Webster's Third New International Dictionary of the English Language, (Principal Copyright 1961) G. & C. Merriam, Springfield, MA. [*Webster^3*]

Journals

[*BLS*] *The Annual Meeting of the Berkeley Linguistics Society*, University of California, Berkeley.

[*CLS*] *Papers from the Regional Meeting, The Chicago Linguistic Society*, The University of Chicago.

[DBR] *Eibeibungaku Ronso (Daito Bunka Review)*, Daito Bunka University.
[EL] *English Linguistics*, The English Linguistic Society of Japan.
[FL] *Foundations of Language*, D. Reidel, Dordrecht, Holland.
Fundamenta Mathematicae, Institute of Mathematics, Polish Academy of Sciences, Warsaw.
[JJG] *Journal of Japanese Grammar*, The Society of Japanese Grammar.
Kiyo (The Bulletin), The College of Literature, Aoyama Gakuin University.
[L&C] *Gengobunka Ronshu (Studies in Languages and Cultures)*, The University of Tsukuba.
[Lg] *Language*, The Linguistic Society of America.
[LI] *Linguistic Inquiry*, MIT Press, Cambridge, MA.
Lingua, North-Holland, Amsterdam.
[ML] *Metropolitan Linguistics*, Tokyo Metropolitan University.
[NLLT] *Natural Language and Linguistic Theory*, D. Reidel, Dordrecht, Holland; Kluwer; Springer.
[ProGM] *Proceedings of the General Meeting*, The English Literary Society of Japan.
[RG] *Eigo Seinen (The Rising Generation)*, Kenkyusha, Tokyo.
Ronshu (The Bulletin), Board of Liberal Arts Education, Aoyama Gakuin University.
[SEGU] *Eigo Gohou-Bunpou Kenkyu (Studies in English Grammar and Usage)*. The Society of English Grammar and Usage.
[SEL] *Studies in English Linguistics*, Asahi Press, Tokyo.
[SIEL] *Studies in English Literature* (English Number), The English Literary Society of Japan.
[SLLL] *Bungei Gengo Kenkyu: Gengohen (Studies in Language and Literature: Language)*, The University of Tsukuba.
[SME] *Kindai Eigo Kenkyu (Studies in Modern English)*, The Modern English Association, Japan.
[TC] *Eibungaku Shicho (Thought Currents in English Literature)*, The English Literary Society of Aoyama Gakuin University.
[TES] *Tsukuba English Studies*, The English Linguistic Society, The University of Tsukuba.
Theoria, John Wiley & Sons, NJ.
[TL] *Theoretical Linguistics*, Walter de Gruyter, Berlin.

Festschrifts, Proceedings and Other Edited Volumes

Anderson, Stephen R. and Paul Kiparsky, eds. (1973) *A Festschrift for Morris Halle*, Holt, Rinehart and Winston, New York.

Bach, Emmon and Robert T. Harms, eds. (1968) *Universals in Linguistic Theory*, Holt, Rinehart and Winston, New York.

Bresnan, Joan, ed. (1982) *The Mental Representation of Grammatical Relations*, MIT Press, MA.

Cacciari, Cristina and Patrizia Tabossi, eds. (1993) *Idioms: Processing, Structure, and Interpretation*, Lawrence Earlbaum, NJ.

References   155

Chiba, Shuji, Akira Ogawa, Yasuaki Fujiwara, Norio Yamada, Osamu Koma and Takao Yagi, eds. (1991) *Gendai Eigogaku no Shoso: Ukaji Masatomo Hakushi Kanreki Kinen Ronbunshu (Aspects of Contemporary English Studies: A Festschrift for Masatomo Ukaji on the Occasion of His Sixtieth Birthday)*, Kaitakusha, Tokyo.

Chiba, Shuji (Editor in Chief), et al., eds. (2003) *Empirical and Theoretical Investigations into Language: A Festschrift for Masaru Kajita*, Kaitakusha, Tokyo.

The English Literary Society of Japan. *Proceedings of the General Meeting [ProGM]*.

Ichikawa, Sanki, ed. (1940) *The Kenkyusha Dictionary of English Philology*, Kenkyusha, Tokyo.

Jackson, Frank, ed. (1991) *Conditionals*, Oxford University Press, Oxford.

Kato, Yasuhiko, ed. (2002) *Proceedings of the Sophia Symposium on Negation*, Sophia University, Tokyo.

Nakau Minoru Kyoju Kanreki-kinen Ronbunshuu Henshuu-iinkai, ed. (2001) *Imi-to Katachi-no Intaafeisu (The Interface between Meaning and Form)*, Kurosio Publishers, Tokyo.

Reuland, Eric J. and Alice G. B. ter Meulen, eds. (1987) *The Representation of (In)definiteness*, MIT Press, Cambridge, MA.

Sano, Tetsuya, Mika Endo, Miwa Isobe, Koichi Otaki, Koji Sugisaki and Takeru Suzuki, eds. (2008) *An Enterprise in the Cognitive Science of Language: A Festschrift for Yukio Otsu*, Hituzi Syobo Publishing, Tokyo.

Shopen, Timothy, ed. (1985) *Language Typology and Syntactic Description II*, Cambridge University Press, Cambridge.

Ukaji, Masatomo, Toshio Nakao, Masaru Kajita and Shuji Chiba, eds. (1997) *Studies in English Linguistics: A Festschrift for Akira Ota on the Occasion of His Eightieth Birthday*, Taishukan, Tokyo.

Ukaji, Masatomo, Masayuki Ike-Uchi and Yoshiki Nishimura, eds. (2003) *Current Issues in English Linguistics*, Kaitakusha, Tokyo.

Books and Articles

Adams, Valerie (1973) *An Introduction to Modern English Word-Formation*, Longman, London.

Akmajian, Adrian (1970) *Aspects of the Grammar of Focus in English*, Doctoral dissertation, MIT. [Published by Garland, New York, 1979].

Baker, Carl L. (1989) *English Syntax*, MIT Press, Cambridge, MA.

Baker, Carl L. (1995) *English Syntax*, 2nd ed, MIT Press, Cambridge, MA.

Ballmer, Thomas T. (1980) "Is Keen an' Faltz keen or false?" *TL* 7, 155–170.

Bolinger, Dwight (1967) "Adjectives in English: Attribution and Predication," *Lingua* 18, 1–34.

Bresnan, Joan (1982) "The Passive in Lexical Theory," Bresnan (ed.), 3–86.

Chafe, Wallace L. (1968) "Idiomaticity as an Anomaly in the Chomskyan Paradigm," *FL* 4, 109–127.

Chomsky, Noam (1965) *Aspects of the Theory of Syntax*, MIT press, Cambridge, MA.

Chomsky, Noam (1995) *The Minimalist Program*, MIT press, Cambridge, MA.

Chomsky, Noam (2013) "Problems of Projection," *Lingua* 130, 33–49.

Chomsky, Noam and Morris Halle (1968) *The Sound Pattern of English*, Harper & Row, New York.

Cole, Peter (1987) "The Structure of Internally Headed Relative Clauses," *NLLT* 5, 277–302.

Comrie, Bernard (1989) *Language Universals and Linguistic Typology*, 2nd ed., University of Chicago Press, Chicago.

Fellbaum, Christiane (1993) "The Determiner in English Idioms," Cacciari and Tabossi (eds.), 271–295.

Fillmore, Charles J. and Paul Kay. (1987) "Construction Grammar Lecture" (A Course Textbook), LSA Summer Institute, Stanford University, Stanford, CA.

Fraser, Bruce (1970) "Idioms within a Transformational Grammar," *FL* 6, 22–42.

Huddleston, Rodney and Geoffrey K. Pullum (2002) *The Cambridge Grammar of the English Language*, Cambridge University Press, Cambridge.

Jackendoff, Ray S. (1973) "The Base Rules for Prepositional Phrases," Anderson and Kiparsky (eds.), 345–356.

Kajita, Masaru (1974) "Henkei Bunpou (Transformational Grammar)," Ota and Kajita, 163–647.

Kajita, Masaru (1977) "Towards a Dynamic Model of Syntax," *SEL* 5, 44–76.

Kajita, Masaru (1983) "Grammatical Theory and Language Acquisition," paper read at a symposium, the 1st Annual Meeting of the English Linguistic Society of Japan.

Kajita, Masaru (1992a) "A Dynamic View of Grammar: Its Conceptual and Empirical Foundations," paper read at Tokyo Circle of English Linguistics, March 28, 1992.

Kajita, Masaru (1992b) "Grammatical Dynamism: A Select Bibliography," Appendix to Kajita (1992a).

Kajita, Masaru (1997) "Some Foundational Postulates for the Dynamic Theories of Language," Ukaji et al. (eds.), 378–393.

Kajita, Masaru (2001) "Seisei-bunpou Tokuron (Advanced Lectures on Generative Grammar)," Tokyo Gengo Kenkyujo (Tokyo Institute for Advanced Studies of Language).

Kajita, Masaru (2002) "A Dynamic Approach to Linguistic Variations," Kato (ed.), 161–168.

Kajita, Masaru (2004) "<Shuhen> <Reigai> wa Shuhen·Reigai-ka (Are "Peripheries/ Exceptions" Really Peripheral/Exceptional?)," *JJG* 4 (2), 3–23.

Kayne, Richard (1994) *The Antisymmetry of Syntax*, MIT Press, Cambridge, MA.

Keenan, Edward (1985) "Relative Clauses," Shopen (ed.), 141–170.

Kiparsky, Paul (1968) "Linguistic Universals and Linguistic Change," Bach and Harms (eds.), 170–202.

Kisseberth, Charles W. (1970) "On the Functional Unity of Phonological Rules," *LI* 1, 291–306.

Kono, Tsuguyo (2013) *Eigo-no Kankeisutsu* (*English Relative Clauses*), Kaitakusha, Tokyo.

Kuroda, Shige-Yuki (1976) "Headless Relative Clauses in Modern Japanese and the

References   157

Relevancy Condition," *BLS* 2, 269–279.

Lakoff, George (1970) *Irregularity in Syntax*, Holt, Rinehart and Winston, New York.

Lakoff, George (1974) "Syntactic Amalgams," *CLS* 10, 321–344.

Lambrecht, Knud (1988) "There was a farmer had a dog: Syntactic Amalgams Revisited," *BLS* 14, 319–339.

Langendoen, D. Terence (1970) "The 'can't seem to' Construction," *LI* 1 (1), 25–35.

Lindström, Per (1966) "First-order Predicate Logic with Generalized Quantifiers," *Theoria* 32, 186–195.

McCawley, James D. (1983) "What's with *With?*" *Lg* 59 (2), 271–287.

McCawley, James D. (1988) *The Syntactic Phenomena of English*, The University of Chicago Press, Chicago.

McCawley, James D. (1993) *Everything that Linguists Have Always Wanted to Know about Logic* *but were ashamed to ask*, 2nd ed., The University of Chicago Press, Chicago.

Mostowski, Andrzej (1957) "On a Generalization of Quantifiers," *Fundamenta Mathematicae* 44, 12–36.

Nagahara, Yukio (1990) *Kankeisetsu (Relative Clauses)*, Taishukan, Tokyo.

Nakau, Minoru (1977) "Eigo ni okeru Huteimeishiku to Hiseigenteki Kankeisetsu (Indefinite NPs and Non-restrictive Relative Clauses in English)," *SLLL* 2, 27–68.

Nakazawa, Kazuo (1983a) "Epenthesis —/t/ Kannyu no Baai—" (Epenthesis: The Case of Excrescent /t/), *RG* 129 (1), 30–31.

Nakazawa, Kazuo (1983b) "Notes on Epenthesis," *L&C* 15, 137–142.

Nakazawa, Kazuo (1991) "Eigo no Shuyobu-Setchu Kankeisetsu (English Head-Internal Relative Clauses)," Chiba et al. (eds.), 351–361.

Nakazawa, Kazuo (1997) "A Note on the Logic of Linguistic Description: A Case of *Kilometer* in American English," Ukaji et al. (eds.), 19–26.

Nakazawa, Kazuo (1999a) "Hasei-teki na Zenchishi-ku (Derivative Prepositional Phrases in English)," *TC* 72, 197–212.

Nakazawa, Kazuo (1999b) "Moderu-no Kenkyuu (Models in Grammatical Dynamism)," *Kiyo (The Bulletin)* 41, 125–134.

Nakazawa, Kazuo (2000a) "Taikei-teki Kuuhaku to Guuzen-no Kuuhaku nituite (On the Dichotomy of Systematic and Accidental Gap)," *Ronshuu (The Bulletin)* 41, 1–4.

Nakazawa, Kazuo (2000b) "Types of Adverbial Noun Phrases in English," *TC* 73, 143–162.

Nakazawa, Kazuo (2001a) "Water Finds Its Level: Derivatives Find General Rules," *TC* 74, 173–189.

Nakazawa, Kazuo (2001b) "Bunpou-ni okeru Kika—Idiomu-no nakano Tougoron-teki Kisokusei—(Grammatical Naturalization: Syntactic Regularity in Idioms)," Nakau Minoru Kyoju Kanreki-kinen Ronbunshuu Henshuu-iinkai (ed.), 449–461.

Nakazawa, Kazuo (2002a) "Epenthesis and a Mode of Extension," *Kiyo (The Bulletin)* 44, 39–46.

Nakazawa, Kazuo (2002b) "The Intensional Qualification of Quantification," *TC* 75,

75-86.

Nakazawa, Kazuo (2003) "Syntax, Semantics and In-Between: In Defense of Predicative," Chiba et al. (eds.), 510-523.

Nakazawa, Kazuo (2004) "Grammatical Naturalization and a Mode of Extension," *TES* 22, 273-278.

Nakazawa, Kazuo (2006a) "Saijoukyuu-ni Michibikareru Kankeisetsu (Relative Clauses Headed by Superlatives)," *SEGU* 13, 111-126.

Nakazawa, Kazuo (2006b) "The Genesis of English Head-Internal Relative Clauses: A Dynamic View," *EL* 23 (2), 380-402.

Nakazawa, Kazuo (2006c) "Sango-fukugougo-no Rizumu-to Shuushokubu-toiu Gainen (Stress Patterns of Three-word Compounds and the Notion 'Modifier')," *ProGM* (The 78th General Meeting), 29-31.

Nakazawa, Kazuo (2007a) "Koubun-kakucho-no Youken (Prerequisites for Construction Extension)" *RG* 152 (12), 747-749.

Nakazawa, Kazuo (2007b) "Kankeisetsu to Doukakusetsu—*Day*-kouzou-o chushin-ni— (Relative Clauses and Appositive Clauses: The Case of *Day* Structure)," *SEGU* 14, 21-36.

Nakazawa, Kazuo (2008) "The Role of Grammatical Dynamism in the Interpretation of Keats' *To Autumn*: Another Case for the Mode of Extension," Sano et al. (eds.), 87-99.

Nakazawa, Kazuo (2014) "Gentei-Shushoku-ni tsuite (On Attributive Modification)," *SEGU* 21, 5-26.

Nakazawa, Noriko (2005) "V-ing: Domeishi to Genzaibunshi no Bunrui o Megutte (V-ing: On the Classification of Gerunds and Present Participles)," *DBR* 36, 49-75.

Nakazawa, Noriko (2006) "There Sesshokusetsu to Kankeidaimeishi no Kenzaika (*There* Contact Clauses and the Emergence of Relative Pronouns)," *SME* 22, 71-91.

Newmeyer, Frederick (1974) "The Regularity of Idiom Behavior," *Lingua* 34, 327-342.

Nunberg, Geoffrey, Ivan A. Sag, and Thomas Wasow (1994) "Idioms," *Lg* 70 (3), 491-538.

Ogawa, Kazuo (1980) *Keats no Ode* (*Keats' odes*), Taishukan, Tokyo.

O'Grady, William (1998) "The Syntax of Idioms," *NLLT* 16, 279-312.

Ota, Akira and Masaru Kajita (1974) *Bunpouron II* (*Grammar II*), Taishukan, Tokyo.

Pulman, Stephen G. (1993) "The Recognition and Interpretation of Idioms," Cacciari and Tabossi (eds.), 249-270.

Quine, Willard Van Orman (1965) *Elementary Logic*, revised ed., Harvard University Press, Cambridge, MA.

Quirk, Randolph, Sidney Greenbaum, Geoffrey Leech and Jan Svartvik (1985) *A Comprehensive Grammar of the English Language*, Longman, London.

Ross, John Robert (1969) "Guess Who?" *CLS* 5, 252-286.

Sakakibara, Hiroaki (1982) "*With*-constructions in English," *SIEL* (English Number)

79-95.

Shimamura, Reiko (1985) "Fukugou-doushi no Katsuyou (Conjugation of Compound Verbs)," *RG* 131 (5), 241.

Suppes, Patrick (1957) *Introduction to Logic*, D. Van Nostrand, Princeton, NJ.

Takonai, Kensuke (1994) "Notes on Internally-Headed Relative Clauses," *ML* 14, 36-50.

Tsubomoto, Atsuro and John Whitman (2000) "A Type of Head-in-Situ Construction in English," *LI* 31, 176-183.

Ukaji, Masatomo (2003) "Subject Zero Relatives in Early Modern English," Ukaji et al. (eds.), 248-277.

Wall, Robert (1972) *Introduction to Mathematical Linguistics*, Prentice-Hall, Englewood Cliffs, NJ.

Williamson, Janis S. (1987) "An Indefiniteness Restriction for Relative Clauses in Lakhota," Reuland and ter Meulen (eds.), 168-190.

Yasui, Minoru (1955) *Onsei to Tsudzuriji* (*Sound and Spelling*), Kenkyusha, Tokyo.

Data Sources
[Corpora]
[*BNC*] *The British National Corpus*. Shogakukan Corpus Network.

[*COCA*] *Corpus of Contemporary American English*. Mark Davies, Brigham Young University.

[*COHA*] *Corpus of Historical American English*. Mark Davies, Brigham Young University.

[*Wordbanks*], [*WBO*] *WordbanksOnline*. Shogakukan Corpus Network.

[Others]
CT: Chicago Tribune. Chicago, Illinois.

DC: The Daily Californian. University of California, Berkeley.

JT: The Japan Times. Tokyo, Japan.

NW: Newsweek. New York, NY.

Sekai Nippou (1993) Tokyo, Japan, December 30, 1993.

WT: The Washington Times (1993) Washington, DC, December 22, 1993.

Beccue, Deborah (1991) *The Daily Californian*, December 5, 1991.

Gates, Bill (1996) "Computer Will Be Chess Champ, but so What?" *The Japan Times*, March 18, 1996.

Graczyk, Wayne (1992) "Baseball Bullet-In," *The Japan Times*, November 6, 1992.

Lane, Charles and Carroll Bogert (1991) "To Market, to Market," *Newsweek*, July 22, 1991.

McPherson, John (1997) A Cartoon, *The Japan Times*, November 9, 1997.

Royko, Mike (1987a) "Some Good Reasons to Keep Walking," *Chicago Tribune*, October 1, 1987.

Royko, Mike (1987b) "Woman Gives Aid and Gets AIDS?" *The Japan Times*, October 30, 1987.

Royko, Mike (1990) "Age is No Asset in U.S. Job Market," *The Japan Times*, August 3, 1990.

Royko, Mike (1994) "Notes from a Right Royal Counseling Session," *The Japan Times*, October 30, 1994.

Schroeder, John (2004) *About the Religion of Senators Kennedy and Kerry: An In-Depth Study of Catholicism...Its Heritage and Beliefs*, Trafford Publishing, Victoria, BC, Canada.

Schwirtz, Mira (1992) "Free Agreement," *The Daily Californian*, January 29, 1992.

Toot, Katie (2011) *Tampa Bay Metro Magazine*.

Index

Authors

A

Adams 92

Akmajian 58

B

Baker 57, 58

Ballmer 24, 45

Beccue 31, 97

Bogert 79

Bresnan 32

C

Chafe 32, 36, 97, 131

Chomsky 19, 25, 40, 42, 46, 48, 105, 128

Cole 52, 53, 71, 72

Comrie 52

D

Duffy 44

F

Fellbaum 36

Fillmore 80

Fraser 32

G

Gates 59, 80

Graczyk 55

H

Halle 19, 25, 40, 42, 46, 48

Hirota 24, 45

Huddleston 67

I

Ichikawa 31

Ito 55, 82

J

Jackendoff 17, 102–104, 122, 124

Jackson 152

K

Kajita 2–4, 9, 15, 28, 29, 32, 37, 38, 60, 65, 72, 99, 104–106, 125, 127–129, 133–135, 138, 152

Kay 80

Kayne 52, 71, 72

Keats 37, 39, 49, 140

Keenan 52, 65

Kiparsky   108
Kisseberth   60
Kono   105
Kuroda   52
L
Lakoff   54, 106, 107
Lambrecht   68
Lane   79
Langendoen   125
Lindström   77
M
McCawley   76, 96, 113, 152
McCready   139, 152
McPherson   59
Mostowski   76
N
Nagahara   53, 54, 56
Nakau   58
Nakazawa, K.   6, 16, 18, 19, 22, 25, 26, 30–33, 37, 44, 51, 74, 81–83, 85, 91, 95, 97
Nakazawa, N.   67–69
Newmeyer   32
Nunberg   31, 32, 36, 97
O
Ogawa   38

O'Grady   36
P
Pullum   67
Pulman   36
Q
Quine   76
Quirk   66, 68
R
Ross   54
Royko   55, 57, 79, 80, 82
S
Sakakibara   113
Schwirtz   59, 79
Shimamura   94
Suppes   76
T
Takonai   53
Tsubomoto   54
U
Ukaji   68
W
Wall   76
Whitman   54
Williamson   57

Terms

A

accidental gap   129, 131, 133, 141–143, 152

accidental hap   131–133, 141, 142, 152

accompaniment   102–104, 111, 112, 117, 118, 123, 124

adverbial (phrase) preposing   118, 120, 121 (cf. preposing)

anaphor   53

antepenult   86–88

argument (in logic)   78, 79, 81, 82, 113, 117

assimilation   20, 27, 92

B

base structure   54, 63, 64

bridge construction   51, 61, 63, 64, 69, 72

C

cause   113–116

circumstantial condition/conditional   104, 112–114, 118–121, 123

clause introducer (CI)   59, 60, 65–67, 69, 71, 82, 130

comparative   60

complementizer   65

conjunction   59, 60

conspiracy   60, 65, 82

construction(al) extension   43, 74, 115, 125

construction-particular characteristics   72, 74

Coref NP   81–84

counter-economical   135

counter-empirical   146

counter-intuitive   135, 146

D

data   2, 6, 25, 51, 66, 67, 69, 72

definite   57, 58, 104, 122

derivative process   3, 4, 25, 152

directional phrase   104, 119, 122–125

domain (in logic)   76

double analysis   51, 60, 61, 63, 64

Dungeon Construction   102–104, 122–126, 131, 134, 142, 144, 145, 151

dynamic model   3, 105, 128

dynamic theory (of grammar)   72

E

ecomony   99

embedded declarative   59

epenthesis   15, 16, 18–28, 33, 44–46

excrescent [t] (/t/)   15, 16, 19–22, 26, 44, 45, 130

existential quantifier   76

explanation   4, 78, 105, 151, 152

extension (→ construction(al) extension, poetic extension, phonological extension, syntactic extension, and transformational extension)

extensional   75, 81, 83

extensional dependency   104, 109, 110, 117

extension format   117, 122–125, 133, 136, 138, 140–145, 147, 150

F

falsifiable/falsifiability   144–147, 152

family   73, 110, 118

family resemblance   49, 50, 56, 60, 67, 72

feeding relation   109

finite   59, 60, 65, 67

functor   76

free relative clause/FRC   57, 58

G

grammar   2, 3, 15, 29, 37, 38, 44, 55, 57, 69, 71, 72, 74, 81–84, 102, 105, 106, 110, 117, 122, 125, 126, 128, 129, 133, 136, 138, 139, 141, 145, 147, 150–152

Grammatical Dynamism   3, 4, 9, 28, 37,

49, 51, 72, 74, 104, 105, 123, 125, 127, 128, 152

Grammatical Naturalization/GN   30–32, 34–36, 46, 97–99, 130, 134–136, 142, 144

H

hapax legomenon   125, 126

head-external interpretation   63, 64

head-external relative clause/HERC   51–53, 56–66, 70–72

head-internal interpretation   51, 60, 63, 64

head-internal relative clause/HIRC   51–58, 60–67, 69–74, 81, 84, 130, 131, 134, 142

hypallage   31

I

impersonal construction   108, 109

indefinite   57, 58, 66, 68, 78

indefiniteness restriction   57

indirect exclamation   59

indirect question   59

instantaneous(ly), instantaneous model   4, 105, 128

instrumental   102–104, 108, 111–113, 123, 145, 151

intensional   74, 75, 77, 78, 83, 84

interrogative WH phrase   77

inverted construction   70, 71

item-specific extension   73, 74

item-specific process   73

K

kakuteiteki context   → referentially fixed context

L

language   2–4, 15, 29, 37, 38, 52, 57, 72, 73, 85, 89, 101, 105, 106, 110, 117, 122, 128–130, 133, 136, 138, 139, 141, 147, 150, 151

language acquisition   4, 15, 38, 73, 105, 128, 147

left-branching structure   52

linguistic theory   2, 3, 125, 151, 152

linguistic universal   57

logical implication   147

'loose' interpretation   27, 106, 139, 140

M

major rule   104, 106–108, 118, 120, 121

Middle English   108, 109

minor rule   104, 106–109, 118, 126

mode of extension   3, 18, 25, 26, 30, 33–36, 44, 46, 48, 49, 140, 152

mother rule   106, 108, 109

mutation   13, 16, 17

N

necessary condition   6, 11, 13–16, 26, 27, 33, 49, 91, 106, 139

necessary provision   152

nonfinite   67, 94, 104, 113, 115, 118, 122, 125

non-instantaneous view   15

O

Old English   108, 109

output-oriented   4, 29, 65, 99, 105, 128, 134

P

passive (transformation/construction)   95, 107–109

penult   86

penultimate   86

phonological extension   110

poetic extension   110

possession   102–104, 111, 112, 123

predicate (n.)   80, 107, 112, 117

predicate (v.)   76, 78

predicate logic   58

predication   76, 77, 84

preposing   120, 124 (cf. adverbial (phrase) preposing)

presentational context   69

Present-Day English   108, 109

Index   165

primary stress   20, 86–89, 99, 134, 135
primitive   75, 84
process-oriented   4, 29, 65, 69, 70, 99,
    100, 105, 128, 135

Q

qualification   57, 74, 84
quantification   74–78, 81, 83, 84
quantified   58, 59, 65–67, 74, 78, 81–84
quantifier   58, 72–74, 76, 78
quantify   73, 74, 76, 78
quantity phrase   77, 78, 83, 84

R

realia   75
reason   113–116
referentially fixed context   58
relative WH phrase   77
relativization   78, 79, 81, 82
relativize   78, 81
restoration   89, 91, 92
right-branching structure   52

S

Sluicing   54
small clause   113, 125
static model   128
stipulation   78
'strict' interpretation   139, 140

structural gap   14
subordinate clause   59, 60, 65, 67
subordinate conjunction   59
subordinate declarative   59
sufficient condition   6, 11, 13, 15, 16, 49,
    91, 106, 139
superlative   56, 57, 60, 64, 65, 72–74, 79,
    81, 82, 130
syntactic extension   32, 110
systematic gap   14

T

tautology/tautological   136, 137, 142, 144,
    146, 150
transferred epithet   30, 31, 134
transformation   106–108
transformational extension   110

U

Universal Grammar   57
universal quantifier   58, 76

V

variable   19, 47, 76

W

WH phrase   77, 78, 83, 84
WH-quantify   81–84
with-construction   110–123, 125

A Dynamic Study of Some Derivative Processes in English Grammar: Towards a Theory of Explanation

著作者　中 澤 和 夫
発行者　武 村 哲 司
印刷所　日之出印刷株式会社

2018 年 10 月 23 日　第 1 版第 1 刷発行©

発行所　　株式会社　開 拓 社

〒113-0023　東京都文京区向丘 1-5-2
電話　（03）5842-8900（代表）
振替　00160-8-39587
http://www.kaitakusha.co.jp

ISBN978-4-7589-2260-9　C3082

JCOPY ＜出版者著作権管理機構 委託出版物＞

本書の無断複製は，著作権法上での例外を除き禁じられています．複製される場合は，そのつど事前に，出版者著作権管理機構（電話 03-3513-6969, FAX 03-3513-6979, e-mail: info@jcopy.or.jp）の許諾を得てください．